# THE SPIRIT OF RUSSIAN ECONOMICS

*By the same author*

THE SPIRIT OF AMERICAN ECONOMICS (Dennis Dobson)

THE STRUGGLE FOR SOUTH AMERICA, Economy and Ideology (Allen & Unwin)

THE JAPANESE IN SOUTH AMERICA, with A. Gerbi (John Day)

ASIA BETWEEN TWO WORLD WARS (Iranian Institute & School of Asiatic Studies)

BRAZIL, A STUDY OF ECONOMIC TYPES (University of North Carolina Press)

*J · F · NORMANO*

# THE SPIRIT OF

# Russian
# Economics

DENNIS DOBSON LIMITED

First published in Great Britain in MCMXLIX by
DENNIS DOBSON LTD, 12 Park Place, St James's,
London SW1. Printed in Great Britain by WEST FIFE
PUBLISHING CO LTD, 34 Bruce Street, Dunfermline
4/R 1950

# Contents

# Foreword

THE development of economic thought in Russia can be compared to a musical fugue. One after another, new voices enter the field, follow one another, co-exist, interrelate, and contribute to the general construction, even through their fights for dominance. In every stage one of the voices is the typical, the leading. English, French, German, and native ideas were the leading voices of this historical fugue in Russia. An investigation of them disclosed the transitional character of the English and French influences, and the persistent increase of the German: especially, German philosophy, which served as a foundation of Russian nativism and anti-Germanism at the same time. The courses of history and of the development of ideas in Russia were less rectilinear, more burdened by traditions, by geography, than in the United States. In no other country was the transplantation and adoption of foreign ideas in the field of economics as strong and rapid as in Russia. The idea of Russian cultural isolation is a myth in the field of economics. No other country so peculiarly re-created foreign economic ideas and attempted to adjust them immediately to its own conditions. No other country fought against imported ideas as violently as Russia. Nowhere else was the national economic thought moving in such a humanistic fog and at the same time continuously attempting practical application of its grandiose schemes. Nowhere else was the theoretical idea of human welfare and happiness so dominant over national elements. *Terra incognita* of the future has always been the happy hunting ground of the Russians, and their search for a new social structure became an intoxication—it was the content of their day-dreams, night dreams, nightmares, drink dreams, and drug dreams. And at the same time the Russians showed themselves masters of realistic national economics. Star-gazers fall so easily into wells. It was not the case this time.

Examination disclosed that even Russian literature is not aware of the more-than-a-century-old struggle of foreign ideas on Russian soil. It became necessary not only to trace the foreign influences but also to confront them with the native currents and

6

follow their fate. We cannot draw a straight balance of payments in the field of ideas. But my investigation shows an outspoken resentment on the part of the great continental Russian economy against the application of English classical insular economics; it traces the spectacular penetration of Russia and Russian economic thought by German ideas, victorious over the French and English; and at the same time the stubborn and finally victorious self-defence of the Russians as Germany became no longer a bridge for, but instead a barrier to, the full development of Russia's productive forces. The study discloses in the case of Russian economics the same ethical character and grand style which permeate Russian belles-lettres, and suggests that Russian economics—similar to American—are more a product of the man in the street than of academic teachings. There are other similarities with the United States: the two continental giants were constantly and feverishly seeking transformation; in both of them the 'transformers' strove for immediate application. But while the English inheritance brought with it to the United States an individualist stamp, the Russian tradition was one of a quest for *sobornost*—this untranslatable term embodying the contrary of Western liberal individualism.[1]

The course of investigation led to a historical study of philosophical, social, and political currents in Russia since the end of the 18th century, as especially in Russia they are inseparable from economic ideas. Literary movements had to be taken into account in view of the social character of Russian literature. In some cases special episodes had to be touched upon as, for instance, Russian peregrinations to Göttingen, meetings with Schelling, and relations with Karl Marx. Excursi on Smithianism and Saint-Simonism had to be inserted. In all cases a parallel discussion of ideas as expressed by the government, the intelligentsia, and the academic profession is presented.

My investigation arrives at the conclusion that in the historical fugue of the evolution of economic ideas in Russia, Bolshevism became a last chord whose harmony crowns the musical fugue. A retrospective analysis of Bolshevism after a quarter of a century of its existence plainly discloses its traditionalism. In its loves and hatreds, longings and recollections, hopes and disappointments, in its words and deeds, Bolshevism is a natural continuation of the Russian intellectual and moral climate; it is the culmination of the economic ideas germinating in Russian soil in the hundred years

[1] Originally *sobornost* meant collective consciousness as seen in Orthodoxy and the village community.

7

preceding the Russian Revolution. The passion of destruction and the grand style of construction, the *furor technicus* which found its early admiration in Russian social Utopias, the idea of the human being daring to make its own history, are old Russian notions. The theory of special ways of Russian history, 'socialism in a single country,' and Bolshevist messianism are also, *mutatis mutandis,* traditional, as well as the Russian historism so in vogue at present in the Soviet Union. Anti-German trends and hatred of the bourgeoisie are traditional and not new features of Bolshevism, no less than its main thought—the primacy of social changes over political—and its lack of interest in individual political and economic freedom. Even the organizational features of the Communist party with its dogmatism and intolerance, instability and fervour, its tendency to rule by coercion for public welfare, appear to be traditional in the history of Russian economic and social thought. Modern Bolshevism is not afraid of the elbowings of the dead. Tradition helps it in attempts at creation of a new universe.

Sometimes one thinks to escape from daily life and to rest in history. But a deep dive—and the strong currents of history bring you back to the present, enlightening you about the genetic interdependence of life and thought. That was my experience in working on this volume. And I admit freely: *Prisca juvent alios. Ego me nunc denique natum gratulor.* Despite the remoteness of some of the periods treated, I found, and the reader probably will find, insights of every kind into the Russia of our day. Knowledge of today's Russia is especially necessary because of its double nature of Wonderland and Looking-Glass World. The Canadian historian James Mavor stated once about Russia that 'no other country offers the student any equal opportunity in a study of economic history,' and added: 'Indeed without taking into account at least the salient features of Russian social development, general economic history cannot be written.'[2] The same observation can be applied to the study of the history of economic ideas in Russia. The great dramas of human life, like those of the Elizabethan theatre, cannot be felt to the full without knowledge also of the stage where they were played. It was difficult within the frame of this volume to offer even a sketch of Russian history. Fortunately for the English reader a few studies have appeared in recent years which can be recommended as background material: two penetrating books by Sir John Maynard,[3] a brief history of Russia by B. H.

[2] James Mavor, *An Economic History of Russia,* London & Toronto, 1914, Vol. I, pp. x-xi.

[3] Sir John Maynard, *Russia in Flux,* London 1941; *The Russian Peasant,* London, 1942.

Sumner [4] and a booklet on modern Russian literature by Ernest J. Simmons.[5]

This little volume presents a link in the chain of my studies in the history of economic thought, being in some respects a companion volume to my *Spirit of American Economics,* and another attempt to call attention to an almost unknown (in Anglo-Saxon countries) stream of thought of a great continental nation. As in my previous book, I beg to be excused from presentation of a formal history: it is again not a description or exposition of books and writers, of hair-splitting theories and definitions, but a view of trends of ideas, for which books and writers are only illustrations. The reader will not find, for instance, in this volume a history of Russian theories of business cycles, in spite of their importance to economic theory. This study, like my *Spirit of American Economics,* is an attempt at a *genetic* investigation of the topic, a lesson in depth. It is, again, a preliminary investigation, preliminary not for scarcity of material—the October Revolution opened the archives, and the yearly printed output is large—but as just the first step in the direction of trapping the spirit of Russian economics. I intend to apply in my presentation the strictest economy of line and to eliminate the unessential, following the principles of a Chinese or a Japanese painting. But the reader must have patience, for, as with a jigsaw puzzle, nothing can be left out of the pattern if the picture is to emerge complete.

The inception of this study goes back more than a quarter of a century when, as a young *Privatdozent,* I started to collect material for this enterprise. In one of the last issues of the Russian liberal newspaper *Retsch* (1918) I published an article on 'The Economic Ideas of Lenin'. My large collection of books and materials in this field remained in Petrograd, but I kept my notes and added new ones during all peregrinations. The new contact with things Russian since my moving in 1941 from Massachusetts to New York with its large Russian community, resulted in an unsuppressible internal urge to continue the investigation and attempt in this way an explanation of 'the riddle of Russian socialism'. This urge forced me even to interrupt a well-advanced work on the economic and social ideas of the Catholic church and give priority to this study.

It is difficult to acknowledge influences and assistance spread over more than a quarter of a century. But I believe that the

[4] B. H. Sumner, *A Short History of Russia,* New York, 1943.
[5] Ernest J. Simmons, *An Outline of Modern Russian Literature,* Cornell University Press, 1943.

seminars of Gerhardt von Schulze-Gaevernitz in Freiburg in Breis-gau and of Peter von Struve in St. Petersburg (both of them masters in the field of Russian economics) probably gave the first stimulus to this work.

In this country my study received encouragement from Professor Wesley C. Mitchell and Professor Robert J. Kerner in connection with our common work in the Russian Economic Institute. Dr Frederick Pollock, Acting Director of the Institute of Social Research, Columbia University, and Dr Felix J. Weil, of the same Institute, were good enough to read the manuscript and, while disagreeing with some of my conclusions, generously offered the benefit of their suggestions. Professor Ernest J. Simmons of Cornell University patiently answered numerous inquiries concerning technical problems that arose in dealing with a Russian topic in the English language. The devoted collaboration of my wife, who shared with me the revival of interest in things Russian, was instrumental in all stages of my work. The American Philosophical Society financially assisted the completion of this study by a grant from the Penrose Fund.

J. F. N.

New York City
June, 1944

# 1. Economics in Russia

THE 19th century was in Western Europe a period of rapid growth and extension of the industrial revolution; of penetration of the capitalist form; of a victorious march of urban ideas and civilization; of their extension into far-off corners of the globe.

Russia, too—late and not always willingly—joined the general trend. But the 19th century was for Russia still a period of hesitation, of intellectual speculation and not of actions. Speaking with the great Russian poet Alexander Blok, a 'humanistic fog' embraced Russia, and it was a period of 'breaking of foreheads against the walls of economic doctrines'.

A forgotten Russian economist, G. Stepanov, correctly observed: 'In no other country but Russia was the study of political economy so approved.' [1]

While in the other regions of un- and underdeveloped capitalism economists and publicists used to write and are still writing poetry (Latin America is typical), in Russia poets, novelists, playwrights were discussing the economic destinies of the world. The Russian intelligentsia during almost the entire 19th century was debating and solving the fate of capitalism, the future of Europe, the decline of the Western civilization; Russia included America in its negative appraisal.[2] Some groups endeavoured to find encouragement and hope in the peculiar features of the old Russian structure and style of life. Russia was striving for a universal solution of all problems.

The tables were turned in the 20th century. Europe began to suffer under a bad spell of pessimism, and Cassandras predicted the end of capitalism, the collapse of Western civilization. Imitators all over the world joined Sombart, Spengler, Keyserling. Nearer to the middle of the 20th century events satisfied Europe that the pessimism was justified, that the end arrived, that the Cassandras

---

[1] G. Stepanov, *Notes on Political Economy*, Kharkov, 1844, Vol. I, p. 10.

[2] The Russian poet of the 19th century, Count Alexey Tolstoy, expressed this opinion in the well-known lines:

We should not look for ideals
And other social principles
In America; America is backward!
Property and capital rule there.

11

were right; dark ages seemed to be the future of mankind. The situation in Russia-U.S.S.R. developed differently in the 20th century. Theoretical discussions were abandoned in favour of economics in action. Russia entered resolutely upon the road of capitalism; but when war and revolution arrested its development in 1914-1918, the U.S.S.R. put industrialization—the substance of the economic process—as its prime goal. The Soviet conception was that the Russian prognosis of the 19th century was correct: Western capitalism was dead or dying, and only Russia was solving the problem of the future social organization. New Russia stopped talking, speculating, and predicting; the pessimism of the 19th century was replaced by the *Sturm und Drang* of a furious activity. New human types appeared on the Russian scene, while the 'superfluous men' and 'unneeded people' of the 19th century died a natural death and their heirs are dying in exile. In a century which more than the eighteenth deserves Hegel's qualification of an excited one, the Russians are working, not discussing. They are endeavouring to repeat on a larger scale and in a faster tempo the West's performance of the 19th century: to industrialize their country; but—in distinction from the Western civilization—not within a capitalistic frame. They claim that the new technology allows short cuts and jumps. The Soviet Revolution passionately and unreluctantly destroyed old Russia and developed a *furor technicus* in the building of a new one.

The immensity of Russia and the fluidity of its boundaries influenced the boundlessness, the breadth of Russian thought reaching out into infinity. The planetary aspects of Russian economic speculations in the 19th century, their totality of thought, have been replaced by an equally grand style and boundlessness of economic action in the 20th. The Russians arrived in the 19th century at the conclusion that the West is rotten and it is useless even to study it. In the 20th century they started to remake their social structure, intending to create a sample, a magnet, an ideal for the rest of the world. In both cases their starting point was idealization: in the 19th century, of the peasant as the bearer and symbol of simplicity and sincerity of life; in the 20th, of the worker—the hero of the reconstruction. In both cases obedience to literary authorities and masters was limitless and unconditional, and the hair-splitting factional fights were of furious temper.

Who were the Russian economists?

The Russian lay economists present a peculiar kaleidoscope of the 'tortured and confined'. Krizânic, one of the pioneers of Pan-Slavism, was imprisoned; emigrants of the 17th century were

Ordyn-Nashchokin and Kotoshikhin; Artem Volynski was tortured; Pososhkov, Novikov, Radishchev were imprisoned and banned; political exiles of the 19th century were numerous.

The persecution of academic social scientists by the government was rather customary throughout the history of Russian universities. Typical was the case of Professor Schad in Kharkov (1816), of Professors Galitch, Arsenyev, Raupach, Plisov, Hermann, and others in Petrograd (1821).[3] During the entire 19th and the beginning of the 20th century the academic careers of many university teachers of social sciences were cut short by administrative dismissal; some of the economists, even, were never permitted to lecture. 'Dismissed from the university' is a frequent last item on rosters of scholars' achievements. Many of them, like Balugyanski and Poroshin, left the university. For some time the government declared philosophy and political economy 'luxury sciences' and eliminated them from the universities' catalogues.

In this way the study of economics was pushed into the underground and the uppperground. In the field of economic thought the bureaucracy and the lay intelligentsia actually outproduced the academic economists; they caused and inspired economic discussions in Russia. The bureaucracy did it in governmental memoranda and actions; many ukases by Peter the Great and Catherine II were lengthy expositions of economic doctrines. The intelligentsia developed their own way of avoiding conspicuousness: they smuggled economic essays into the so-called thick monthlies—a specifically Russian institution—periodicals where novels, poetry, literary criticism, and popular science mingled with discussions of abstract philosophy and economic problems. The novel itself in Russia was often of a pronounced economic and social character. Not only Chernyshevski in *What To Do* or Turgenev in *Fathers and Sons* and *The Virgin Land,* but also Nekrasov, Saltykov-Shchedrin, and many *dei minores* injected economic theories into their writings. Especially the *Narodniki* created a school of social novelists—a parallel to the early Bolshevik novel of the 20th century. While the bureaucracy was as a rule more concrete, and exercised actual and immediate influence on economic policy, the

---

[3] Under the influence of the curator Runich the University Court declared the teachings of Hermann and his follower Arsenyev dangerous to the welfare of the state. The use in classrooms of previously published works by Hermann (*A Brief Guide Book to a General Theory of Statistics* and *General Theory of Statistics esp. of the Russian State*), by Galitch (*History of Systems of Philosophy*), and by Arsenyev (*Sketch of Statistics of the Russian State*), was prohibited and the books were ordered to be withdrawn from the libraries.

13

intelligentsia lived in a humanistic fog of fine distinctions, blind and fanatical following of the masters, and intense factional fights. Names of periodicals like *Messenger of Europe, Russian Wealth, God's World,* and *Russian Thought* meant battle cries to the Russian intellectual.

Economic conceptions thus were discussed all over the immense space of the Russian Empire. But generally speaking, economics led in Russia a distinctly underground life during a large part of the 19th century.

The growing capitalist development of the late 19th century brought into the larger national scene professional academic economists: research workers in touch with Western technique and methods of investigation. Not only St. Petersburg and Moscow, the older centres of economic study, but the provincial universities too, especially Kiev, Kazan, and Kharkov, underwent a westernization process in the teaching of economics. More or less at the same time vested interests previously working in individual isolation began to organize their representation, strengthen their positions, and seek a theoretical foundation of their desires and intentions.

The popular attitude toward the academic discipline of political economy was not very favourable in Russia. The discussion between the poet and the jester in Alexander Blok's fragment, *Dialogue on Love, Poetry and Civil Service,* represents an echo of the common resentment of the conflict between common sense and political economy.

The intelligentsia was the bridge between public opinion and revolutionary economics. The socialist teachings of the Russian revolutionaries often deeply affected the ways of thinking and the beliefs of future bureaucrats, academic teachers, and publicists, as well as the growing layer of the Russian reading public. The intelligentsia was the bridge to 'the people', to the masses, to the peasant, to the worker.

Of course, there was not a straight separation of groups, as there was not, generally speaking, any watertight isolation of classes in old Russia. Conservative bureaucracy, liberal intelligentsia, revolutionary socialists—they were communicating vases, mutually influencing and influenced. Emperor Alexander I and the future Emperor Nicholas I conferred with Robert Owen; the Saint-Simonists Count Reutern and Admiral Greig were ministers of finance; Count Speranski surrounded himself with German liberal professors of Smithian trend; most of the eternal *Privatdozents* were socialists. I think Prince Vyazemski's statement that 'in

14

periods of reaction there has been in Russia no society, only population' is not correct: there always have been thoughtful groups in Russia. More, even: they were not satisfied that their meditations be of an abstract, theoretical character only.[4]

How did the fundamental change between the 19th and 20th centuries' economic climates actually occur in Russia?

It occurred as a result of struggle of ideas, native, quasi-native, and imported : of world waves and of local currents representing or pretending to represent national and group interests. The world waves, in reaching Russian soil despite all the barriers and frontiers, often took on rather unexpected, fantastic forms. We notice a constant fight of imported ideologies—English, French, German—on Russian soil. In their struggle for Russian markets, raw materials, and political influence, the competing nations used ideological weapons, and the Russian bureaucracy and intelligentsia, equally susceptible in reception and imitation, willingly became influenced. But even the genuine native Russian theories attempting the defence against imported ideologies, adorning them in picturesque national clothes, trying to save the Russian-Slavic national face, the old Russian social features, constantly dreaming of messianic offensives —even these currents in their effort to cover up, to defend Russian economic backwardness by making a virtue of it, even they found their inspiration and wisdom in foreign sources.

Pushkin emphasized in his *Sketches on Literature* how after Peter the Great 'European influence expanded all over Russia . . . Holland and England created our fleet, Prussia and France our army, Leibnitz designed the plan of our civil organization'; and Danilevski, speaking of Russian currents and ideologies, equally accused the aristocracy, the democratic constitutionalists, and the nihilists of attempting to 'imitate Europe and producing just caricatures'.[5]

The early Russian 'economists' do not show traces of foreign influence. The *House-Orderer* by Silvester Medvedev which appeared in the 16th century was a picture of household economy in his time and a collection of household rules.

In the 17th century Grigori Kotoshikhin's *On Russia During the Reign of Alexey Mikhailovitch*, written in exile in Stockholm, is at its best in the description of the immediate surroundings of the Tsar. The Croat Yuri Krizanic combined a peculiar mercantilist

[4] Similarly P. N. Milyukov emphasized " striving at usefulness " as a feature of early Russian historians. *The Main Currents of Russian Historical Thought*, Moscow, 1898, Vol. I, p. 164.

[5] Danilevski, *Russia and Europe*, St. Petersburg, 1895 edition, pp. 313-315.

theory of Pan-Slavic absolutism with insistence on a union with the Roman Catholic church and some physiocratic tenets: A. L. Ordyn-Nashchokin (middle of the 17th century), whom Klyuchevski considered the first Russian economist, favoured 'self-administration at that period, admired Western Europe, and complained about 'extreme nausea' in Moscow. Artem Volynski was the author of an *Instruction to Manage an Estate*. All of them, even the first Russian mercantilist of the transition from the 17th to the 18th century, the merchant of peasant origin, Ivan Pososhkov, author of a *Book on Poverty and Wealth*, certainly drew their knowledge and conclusions from observation of the Russian actuality and not from foreign literary sources.[6] Pososhkov anticipated the statement *pauvre paysan, pauvre royaume* when he said: 'In whatever kingdom people are rich, the kingdom is rich; in whatever kingdom people are poor, that kingdom cannot be rich.'[7] Like the mercantilists, he put emphasis on trade ('trade is a great thing'); he anticipated Knapp's state theory of money and in a picturesque way expressed the nominalist doctrine: 'His most Illustrious Majesty's word is so valid with us, that if His Majesty orders "ruble" engraved on a copper piece, it will circulate in trade and remain unchanged [in its value] forever . . . . We are not like the foreigners.'[8]

Curiously enough, Peter the Great, who was forced by financial problems to adopt mercantilist principles in a milieu of natural economy, in a country whose political development in foreign relations outstripped its economic progress, failed to see an ally in Pososhkov—the Moscow merchant-progressivist whose mercantilist teachings included some physiocratic elements rather natural under Russian conditions.

One of the very few writers on historico-economic problems who showed knowledge of and interest in European literature was the historian of the 18th century Prince Michel Shcherbatov; he shifted from the field of history to *cameralia* of the German type. In his

6 When Professor M. P. Pogodin became first acquainted with Pososhkov's *Book on Poverty and Wealth*, he felt fortunate in his discovery of a Russian autodidact who " being born 50 years prior to the origin of political economy in Europe, vividly understood its rules " and in many respects was the predecessor of Adam Smith. See Pogodin's Foreword to *Pososhkov's Works*. Moscow, 1842, Vol. I, p. viii.

7 A similar statement was made by Kotoshikhin: " Where common people are numerous and rich, the rulers and boyars are also rich and powerful."

8 We find a similar statement in Karamzin's criticism of Speranski's *Financial Plan:* " If the Emperor would give us stamped chips and order them to be put in circulation instead of rubles (of course, finding ways to prevent counterfeiting), we would take them."

Utopia, *Description of the Ofirland,* opposing the reforms of Peter the Great, he claimed to be following Western experience, and evidently was influenced by Montesquieu.

The true penetration of foreign economic ideas into Russia began in the last quarter of the 18th century.

# II. English Influence

But he was well-read in Adam Smith
And was a deep economist.

PUSHKIN, *Eugene Onegin.*

RELATIONS between Russia and England are of old standing. As early as the 16th century the English 'Society for the Discovery of Unknown Lands' formed a Russian company.[9] Ivan the Terrible was called the English Tsar. Of English influence on Russian culture, an excellent account is presented by Ernest J. Simmons' study.[10] The end of the 18th and beginning of the 19th century in old Russia witnessed a 'blitz' penetration of English influence in Russian economic thought.

The brief enthusiasm for English institutions shown by Catherine II was the expression of the contemporary European Anglomanias; it was inspired in Russia by the French Encyclopedists. Catherine the Great sent Russian students to Oxford, Cambridge, and Glasgow; and even from Germany, Russian students returned under the spell of England.

Alexander N. Radishchev, the future father of Russian liberalism, who as a seventeen-year-old boy was sent by Catherine the Great to study at the University of Leipzig (at the same time as Goethe), returned to Russia full of admiration for England. His ode 'On Liberty' is a eulogy of Cromwell and Washington; his famous *Journey from St. Petersburg to Moscow* was obviously inspired by English liberal ideas.

The French Revolution caused a pro-English reaction in the government, and Napoleon's invasion a similar reaction in the young Russian intelligentsia. Russia became the granary of Europe and especially of England during the Napoleonic Wars, and Alexander I appeared a faithful ally of England. Economic ties between the countries became important. In 1807 Savary reported to Napoleon from Petrograd that half of the 1,200 boats yearly enter-

[9] A. Francis Stewart, *Scottish Influence in Russian History*, Glasgow, 1913.
[10] Simmons, *English Literature and Culture in Russia (1553-1840)*, Cambridge, Mass., 1935.

18

ing the Neva flew the British flag. The merchants of that period
in Russia were Englishmen or Germans, trading with England.
The landlords were tributaries of England: selling lumber and
buying luxury objects. England supplied the nobility with cloth
for their uniforms, furniture for their homes, dishes for their tables
—everything, including paper, pen points, and ink, came from
England. In Pushkin's words:

> What London haberdashers hallow
> We buy with timber and with tallow.

As Simmons aptly summarizes, 'All the people of consequence
were members of the English Club in Moscow, which appears to
have been modelled after the London coffee-house. English manufactured goods flooded the country. Onegin equipped his house
with English furnishings, ate roast beef, and dressed in the latest
fashion as a London dandy. Indeed, when Pushkin's famous hero
is out of sorts, he is described as afflicted with English spleen.'[11]
Speaking in the style of the period, the French *petit-maître* was
at that time replaced by the English dandy. 'One can well imagine
that Pushkin was not exaggerating when he described Muromski
in his tale *Baryshnya-Krestyanka* [*La Demoiselle-Paysanne*] as an
Anglomaniac who planted an English garden, had his groom wear
English livery, hired a governess to give his daughter English
lessons, and farmed his land on the English system.'[12] Byron conquered Russian youth, and Childe Harold became its idol. Pushkin's *Eugene Onegin* and Griboyedov's *Woe from Wit* are illustrations of this transition from French to English influence.

It was a period of admiration for and imitation of the English
system of agriculture. Russian landlords engaged English farm
overseers, introduced English cattle and equipment. A monument
to Arthur Young was erected in the village Voronovo of Podolsk
County, Moscow Province. In 1807 Young's son visited the more
advanced estates in Russia, collecting economic and statistical data.

The Moscow Society of Agriculture (founded in 1818) concentrated and spread the agricultural Anglomania. It developed a
decidedly practical activity in contrast to the more theoretical Imperial Free Economic Society of St. Petersburg. Its publication, the
*Agricultural Journal*, specialized in translations of English studies.
Count Rostopchin, author of the anonymous pamphlet *Iron and
Wooden Plough* of 1806, declared that in Russia 'English agriculture decorates the landscape, but the unsophisticated Russian serf
economy based on correct economic calculation enriches.'

[11] *Ibid.*, p. 240.          [12] *Ibid*, p. 85.

19

In the field of social sciences English influence manifested itself in the popularity of Bentham's philosophy and Adam Smith's economic teachings.

Benthan captured Russian minds. Dumont, the French translator of his works and collaborator of Mirabeau, went to Russia in 1802 and wrote in 1808 that there were as many translated copies of Bentham sold in Russia as originals in London. Dumont was elected correspondent on political economy by the University of Kharkov.

Translation of Bentham was begun in 1804 by the official *St. Petersburg Journal*, Speranski participating. In 1805-06 appeared two volumes published by order of the Tsar, and in 1811 the third volume.

No less important than the translations of his works were the personal relations Bentham established when he came to Russia in 1786 to visit his brother. N. Pypin devoted a special study to this subject.[13] The most interesting chapter in the story of these relations was the one with Mordvinov. The intermediary was Samuel Bentham, the brother of Jeremy, for some time the administrator of Potemkin's estates in White Russia. He was an old acquaintance of Mordvinov and at his return to England received from Mordvinov for Jeremy Bentham a copy of the French translation of G. M. Jovellanos' *Identité de l'Interêt Individuel*, published in 1806 in Petrograd by order of Prince Kochubei.[14]

A spread of interest in economic problems is clearly noticeable in the Russian society of the early 19th century. An anonymous pamphlet appeared in Moscow in 1815 under the title *Answer of a Russian Citizen to the Question: Is It Useful to Establish and Spread Manufactures in Russia?* Its foreword emphasized the general interest in problems of Russia's economic future, and the growing discussion of 'manufactures'. Books by French and English writers, fashionable at that time, demanding political freedom for industrial development, 'penetrated to the most far-off provincial towns'.[15]

---

[13] In *Messenger of Europe* (1869).

[14] V. S. Ikonnikov, *Count Mordvinov*, Petrograd, 1873, p. 73. Gaspar M. de Jovellanos belonged to the small group of reformers in the reign of Charles III in the second half of the 18th century. He represented the laissez-faire current and shared the physiocratic trend of the opinions of Conde de Campomanes. Bentham's last letter to Russia was addressed to Mordvinov in 1830; in it he introduced the South American general Santander, who was spending his exile in Europe.

[15] V. Semevski, *Political and Social Ideas of the Decembrists*, Petrograd, 1909, p. 66.

The economic discussions were in line with the teachings of Adam Smith 'fashionable among the young people' (to quote the author of the above-mentioned 1815 pamphlet).

Pushkin's famous lines state most significantly of the youth of the period that

> He talked about the wealth of nations;
> The state relied, his friends were told,
> Upon its staples, not on gold.[16]

The main ideas of Adam Smith's *Wealth of Nations* were known in Russia prior to the publication of the work in England (1776). Two professors at the University of Moscow, Desnitski and Tretyakov, studies in 1768 in Glasgow under Adam Smith, and Tretyakov's *Consideration of the Cause of Abundance and of Slow Enrichening of the State in Ancient as well as Modern Nations,* based on his Glasgow notes, appeared in 1772. But only after the brief period of Catherine II's flirtation with the French philosophers did Smithianism become for a time the dominating and official current of thought in Russia. It is mentioned in Russian literature that Adam Smith among other scholars was a frequent visitor of the sister of Count A. Vorontsov, the Countess Dashkov, whose son studied at the University of Edinburgh.[17] There were probably other personal contacts, but the first propagandists of Smithianism in Russia were, of course, the two Vorontsovs, Count A. and Count S., both ambassadors to London, of whom Simmons writes:

' . . . The love of the two Vorontsov brothers for England may fairly be described as an Anglomania.

'The elder, Count A. Vorontsov, remained in England as ambassador only a short time (1762-64), but almost twenty years later, when his brother, Count S. Vorontsov, took over the same post, he wrote to him: "There is no people who in private life is more virtuous, moral, and hospitable than they; it is fine to live and be born there." Indeed, A. Vorontsov, after his return to Russia, lost none of his interest in England. He was continually receiving news of the country from his brother and from English books, such as *The Wealth of Nations,* which, after reading them, he sent to Radishchev, another admirer of England, who was in exile in Siberia.

---

[16] Pushkin's writings, especially his *Eugene Onegin,* present an encyclopedia of contemporary Russian life, its economic history, ideas, and observations. An investigation of Pushkin's economic ideas would be a worth-while but a difficult task. I hope some day to devote time to this topic.

[17] Ikonnikov, *op. cit.,* pp. 76-77. The young Dashkov passed his examination in 1779 with great success.

The influence of Vorontsov's knowledge of English political institutions on the reforms which he advocated at the beginning of the reign of Alexander I may be clearly detected.

'S. Vorontsov was a deep student of English political and economic thought and in his voluminous correspondence with relatives and friends in Russia he kept them informed of contemporary developments in English life and culture. In this he was instrumental in disseminating English influence. To take one important instance: Vorontsov was a great admirer of the writings of Adam Smith, and upon hearing that his Emperor was contemplating a new tariff law, he wrote to his brother, who was close to Alexander I, "to read, reread, and learn by heart the book of Adam Smith, *The Wealth of Nations*". From further remarks in his correspondence it is easy to see that S. Vorontsov had made a study of Smith and his predecessors in economic theory.'[18]

In his liberal period Alexander I was completely under the influence of Bentham and Adam Smith; translations of their works were made on the Emperor's orders and printed in official publications. The first complete translation of *The Wealth of Nations* was undertaken under government orders by the vice-governor of Chernigov, N. R. Politkovski, who was paid 5,000 rubles for this service. The translation appeared in four parts in St. Petersburg in 1802-1806.

Alexander I supported financially some of Robert Owen's experiments [19] and anxiously followed everything progressive in his time. He was enthusiastic, for instance, about Pestalozzi. There was a lively correspondence between the Tsar and Jefferson.

The minister of commerce, Count N. P. Rumyantsev, and the unofficial cabinet of Alexander I—the famous trio Novosiltsev, Kochubei (both studied in England), and Czartoryski—were admirers of Adam Smith.

At this period the banned Radishchev was returned to work on legislative projects.

The Smithian trend strongly influenced the great Russian statesman Count M. M. Speranski. Married to an Englishwoman, a friend of Bentham's brother; for some time the closest and most trusted advisor of Alexander I; later arrested, and exiled in 1812; again returned to St. Petersburg, entrusted by Nicholas I with the codification of Russian laws; Speranski was full of contradictions and conflicts, like the period in which he lived. As one of his

18 Simmons, *op. cit.*, pp. 96-98.
19 The grand duke Nicholas Pavlovitch visited New Lanark and suggested to Robert Owen that he migrate to Russia with his workers.

biographers remarked, Speranski knew Russia 'from the hut to the throne'. [20] Following 'the course of my imagination', to use his own words, Speranski introduced various advanced notions into the Russian administration. His *Plan* was more modest than the liberal programme of the first part of the reign of Alexander I. It was opposed by the majority of the landed nobility, whose objections were best expressed in the famous *Exposé on Old and New Russia* by the great historian Karamzin. In his early administrative work Speranski attempted to introduce constitutionalism into Russia; but in his later career, as chairman of the Supreme Criminal Court, he signed the death verdict against the Decembrists.

Speranski's group of collaborators was composed of Smithians, many of them imported from Western Europe. The most prominent among them were M. A. Balugyanski, the future dean of the faculty of law and the first rector of the University of St. Petersburg, and L. H. Jacob, both of them admirers and followers of English economics, of the laissez-faire ideas of the period, of the entire conception of the growing individualist liberalism. We shall make better acquaintance of this group in Chapter IV. They participated in the codification of Russian legislation; they, especially Balugyanski, were instrumental in the preparation of the famous *Financial Plan* of 1810. But even the 1803 draft prepared by Speranski was based on English ideas. Novosiltsev asked the Emperor to assign Baron V. I. Steingel (the future Decembrist) to assist him in his work on 'adjustment of the English Constitution to Russia'. [21] The very pillar of Smithianism among Speranski's collaborators was the famous Admiral Count N. S. Mordvinov, who also participated in the elaboration of the *Financial Plan*. In this way Adam Smith's ideas penetrated into Russian legislation.

The liberal N. I. Turgenev and the conservative Admiral Count N. S. Mordvinov were the two Russian economists representative of the period. The house of Turgenev's family in Moscow was a great cultural centre, a meeting place of German professors, Russian writers, and the entire intelligentsia. The economist's father, I. P. Turgenev, was a member of the famous liberal Novikov's circle, one of the contributors, translators, and editors of the Friendly Scientific Society, organized by Novikov. He was exiled in connection with Novikov's case, but became the director of the University of Moscow under Emperor Paul I. His son N. I.

[20] M. V. Dovnar-Zapolski, *Political Ideals of M. M. Speranski*, Moscow, 1905.
[21] *Social Movements in Russia in the First Half of the 19th Century*, St. Petersburg, 1905, Vol. I, p. 286.

Turgenev was a friend of Pushkin and of Prince A. I. Odoyevski, of Pushkin's professor A. P. Kunitsyn (who was dismissed in 1821 from the lyceum of Tsarskoye Selo), of the entire young enlightened aristocracy of the period. N. I. Turgenev, who, like all the sons of I. P. Turgenev, was considered in Moscow a 'notorious German', represented a typical case of transplantation of English ideas to Russia via Germany. He studied at the University of Göttingen. We are going to examine later the great role of this university in the development of ideas in Russia, only noting here that Göttingen was at that period one of the strongest nuclei of Smithianism on the European continent. 'Smith delights me', wrote the young Turgenev in Göttingen, 'and this science will be my main occupation, I believe, during all my life'.[22]

Wilhelm Roscher correctly observed that Adam Smith did not at first make much of an impression in Germany. But at the beginning of the 19th century the group around Freiherr von Stein were enthusiastic Smithians. Like von Stein, Turgenev studied at Göttingen and, like von Stein, he was an admirer of Adam Smith.

N. I. Turgenev participated in the German liberal movement both as a university student and later as one of von Stein's assistants in his administration of Prussian territories reoccupied by the Russians. He collaborated with Mordvinov in the Departments of Economy and of Civil and Ecclesiastic Affairs, and with Speranski in the Department of Law and Legislation. Under the minister of finance Guryev, Turgenev served as the learned secretary of a section where Balugyanski was chairman and Jacob one of the members.

Turgenev's *Essay on the Theory of Taxation* (1818) is a quintessence of economic liberalism and free trade theories. On the cover of the first edition one reads: 'The author, assuming all the expenses connected with the printing of this book, offers all the proceeds of its sales for the benefit of peasants imprisoned for arrears in taxes'.

Admiral Count N. S. Mordvinov, member of the State Council, president of the Imperial Free Economic Society in St. Petersburg, was of a different type. As Turgenev represented the Russian liberal intelligentsia, Mordvinov personified the enlightened Russian conservative bureaucracy at its best, with a distinct aristocratic colouring. Bentham considered Mordvinov 'the head of some kind of opposition' in Russia and wrote that through his 'agent' Mordvinov he approached Alexander I (in 1814). Admiral Mordvinov's

[22] N. I. Turgenev, *Diaries and Letters* (Archive of the Turgenev Brothers, I), p. 243.

'opinions' were distributed in hundreds of handwritten copies and made him popular all over the empire.

While Turgenev spoke as an *homme de culture*, Mordvinov was first of all a statesman. 'Mordvinov, the follower of Bentham, was just as rightly placed in the chair of the Department of Civil and Ecclesiastical Affairs of the Council of State as Mordvinov, the follower of Adam Smith, presiding over the Department of Economy'.[23] Mordvinov's efforts and achievements in the field of scientific agriculture, and his insistence on the necessity for organized collection of statistical data as the basis for administration, deserve a special and thorough investigation. Mordvinov made studies in England in 1774-1777; he visited America; he married an Englishwoman; he corresponded with Bentham; his reserved style of life was English in character. He was the Alexander Hamilton of Russia, and this comparison is even more striking than that of Lomonosov with Benjamin Franklin.[24] Mordvinov and Hamilton—both followers of Adam Smith—realized the peculiarities of their great continental countries which made inadvisable most of the practical applications of the classical theories; they also were alike in their emphasis on and propagandizing of the national standpoint. They were precursors of the national current in the economic thought of their countries; they represented the trend later on traditionally tied up with Friedrich List's name. Mordvinov opposed Storch, who claimed that Russia was inevitably dependent on other (industrial) nations. He was a protectionist who would approve free trade if it were universal. But he considered English free trade ideas unacceptable for the Russia of his time.[25] Russia suffered heavily under Napoleon's blockade of England. Laissez faire and non-interventionism were the hope of her landowners. Mordvinov's propaganda for credit organization and his belief in its creative power anticipated the later theories of McLeod.

Typically along the lines of the early English classical economists Mordvinov exclaimed: 'Grant freedom to thought, to working heads, to all intellectual and physical qualities of a man. . . . . Degree of freedom is the degree of acquired wealth. Establish public welfare on the foundation of individual welfare'.[26]

As early as 1801 Mordvinov began to elaborate plans for and urge the establishment of banks following 'the Scotch example'.

---

[23] V. S. Ikonnikov, *Count Mordvinov*, Petrograd, 1873, p. 348.
[24] Cf. Normano, *The Spirit of American Economics*, Dennis Dobson, 1946, p. 37.
[25] See N. S. Mordvinov, *Some Considerations on the Subject of Manufactures in Russia and on the Tariff*.
[26] *Collected Opinions of N. S. Mordvinov*, Vol. III, p. 281.

His *Considerations on Banks* had several editions and provoked lively discussion. It was translated into French and reviewed in Italy. We know that Mordvinov sent copies of the French translation of the second Russian edition, *Réflections sur les banques*, to several European economists, J. B. Say and Charles Ganilh at the head of the list. His *Some Considerations on the subject of Manufactures in Russia and on the Tariff* (1815; French translation, 1816) vividly reminds one—and not by the title only—of Alexander Hamilton. Mordvinov advocated a harmonious development of productive forces; he appears as an outspoken industrialist and protectionist. He stressed that if Russia did not want to remain behind all other nations and wished to retain her place in Europe, the country must—even if slowly—move from the agricultural to the manufacturing and handicraft stage. While insisting on popular initiative, Mordvinov regarded the nobility as the proper administrators of the Russian economy, especially of the banks. He sought new markets for Russia. In a memorandum of 1816 he discussed *Ways and Means to Keep the Allegiance of the Caucasian Peoples*.

The conservative statesman Mordvinov lacked sometimes in his writings (but not in his actions) the humanitarianism of the liberal Turgenev. Mordvinov claimed that the emancipation of peasants could begin only after the development of industry and of sufficient labour supply for the landlords; in that case 'slavery will automatically disappear, as it will be clear to everybody that it does not pay'. Mordvinov's economic theory contrasted with the humanist views and feelings of an emotional and enlightened intellectual like Turgenev. They debated this problem at length, and the following exchange of remarks is typical: 'In your eyes all serfs are of course saints and all landlords tyrants', said Mordvinov. 'You are almost correct', was Turgenev's reply.

Smithianism penetrated the periodicals of this epoch. Tugan-Baranovski, who gave special attention to periodicals in his historical study of the Russian factory,[27] was puzzled by the fact that Adam Smith's ideas were preached in the official journal of the Ministry of Interior:

'Official authors describe Adam Smith as a great man, admit that he discovered "the great truth". They stress that the role of the government is not to act but just not to hinder, and to protect the natural freedom of industry. The minister of interior Kochubei in his report for 1803 formulated the programme of the government in the following way: To leave private industry alone; to possess

[27] M. I. Tugan-Baranovski, *The Russian Factory in Past and Present*, St. Petersburg, 1907, pp. 264 f.

as much as possible concise data of its development; to provide the proper assistance in case of need; especially to eliminate all handicaps;—these are the general rules of this part of administration.'

Smith's teachings were presented in the official *St. Petersburg Journal* in 1803 and in the *Statistical Journal* in 1808 (by Balugyanski). Translations of Smithianists like the Swiss economist Herrenschwand and of works by Alexander Hamilton were offered by the government to the Russian public. The official *St. Petersburg Reports* adopted a similar position and were outspokenly in favour of free trade at that period.

Some of the Russian followers of Adam Smith of the next decade not only accepted the laissez-faire doctrine in regard to trade but extended it literally to the agrarian social structure, opposing the idea of governmental intervention in the question of slavery. A typical example was the agrarian and free trade weekly the *Spirit of Journals* (1815-1820), which continuously attacked Mordvinov and especially his bank projects.

Carrying translations of European economists like Say, Sismondi, and others, this weekly contained many original contributions on the above questions. Sympathies for the Western European ideas of Adam Smith and later of Sismondi were combined with a devotion to the national institution of serfdom. The *Spirit of Journals* was in favour of small landlords' factories. Borrowing the vocabulary of the Western critics of large capitalistic factories, it often compared the situation of the factory worker in England unfavourably with that of a Russian peasant.

The liberalism of Alexander I was a short-lived episode. Speranski's constitutional reform along 'English' lines failed to materialize. The Emperor himself, after his return from Europe, came more and more under the spell of a religious mysticism, and his administration become the head of European reaction. The philosophy of 'free thinking' and 'Voltairianism' gave way to religious trends. The reaction started as a literary movement: Admiral Shishkov delivered his address 'Discussion of the Love of Fatherland' before the conservative society *Besieda* (Friends of Russian Letters) in 1811. It led to a political fight against 'the rotten ideas of the West', to admiration of the 'customs and virtues of the fathers' (as emphasized by Sergei Glinka in the *Russian Messenger)* and to N. M. Karamzin's statement: 'We have no devotees of high learning', in his *Exposé on Old and New Russia*.

The Russian intelligentsia represented at that time by the young officers of the Imperial Guard, their observations in Europe still

27

fresh in memory, became the bearers of the banner of liberalism.[28] In one of his unfinished stories Pushkin remarked that among the officers of 1818 in St. Petersburg 'strictness of rules and political economy' were in vogue.

Impressed by the forms and ideas of the French Revolution, this youth was also influenced by the current of economic liberalism as represented by Bentham and Smith. One of the Decembrists, Baron V. I. Steingel, stated that the government's sponsoring translations of foreign books in the field of politics and economics, its publicizing of the fundamentals of the English constitution and so on, offered a certain stimulus to the conspiracy.

The tradition of secret societies was always strong in Russia. They flourished especially in the times of Peter I, Elizabeth, and Catherine II. The popularity of Masonic lodges in Russia, and acquaintance with conspiratory political groups in Western Europe —personal connections with the *Carbonari,* with the order of *Illuminates,* with the Prussian *Tugendbund*—were of influence in Russian development. All Europe in the early 19th century was full of secret societies, especially Germany, Italy, Spain, Greece. The trend was strengthened in Russia by the numerous literary groups not only in St. Petersburg and Moscow but even in several provincial centres. The twenties and thirties especially were blossom time for the literary salons of the Russian aristocracy, among which *Arzamas* is the most famous because of its connection with Pushkin's name. But the salons of Princess Zinaida Volkonski, A. Elagina, Prince V. F. Odoyevski, and Count V. Sollogub also left their impression on the development of Russian culture. While discussions of aesthetics, literature, and philosophy dominated, questions of politics and economics were touched upon. In itself the fact of secret gatherings was important for Russia's development.[29] Griboyedov ridiculed them in his *Woe from Wit,* making Repetilov reveal:

> We're a Society. We hold a secret meeting
> Each Thursday. It's a very private league.

The history of the Decembrists is rather well known. The movement originated as a kind of combination of numerous local

[28] Cf. M. Gershenson, *P. Y. Chaadayev,* St Petersburg, 1908, p. 2.
[29] Cf. M. Aronson and S. Reiser, *Literary Circles and Salons,* Leningrad, 1929. N. I. Turgenev and A. P. Kunitsyn undertook the attempt to form in St. Petersburg in 1818 a political Society of the Nineteenth Year of the Nineteenth Century in which they offered membership to Pushkin. Cf. Alexander Fomin, *On the History of the Problem of Development of Social Ideas in Russia at the Beginning of the 19th Century,* Moscow, 1915.

initiatives which took shape after the end of 1816, and came to its climax and explosion in the miscarried revolt of 1825.

The Decembrist movement combined admiration for English laissez faire and infatuation with the ideas of the French Revolution; it originated as a protest against the reactionary trend of the second part of the rule of Alexander I. Sources and motives were varied; the movement was of a rather complicated and not uniform nature. It was influenced and fertilized by personal observations, academic lectures, literary currents, and the *Zeitgeist*.

Of course, the residence of Russian officers in France was of importance, but one can also trace some influence from Spain and Naples. Adam Smith was admired; but Sismondi was also read and Destutt Tracy known (especially his *Commentaire sur l'ésprit des lois);* The Americans Hamilton and Jefferson were noted, and the ideas of American federalism aroused curiosity. The regimental libraries contained works by Benjamin Franklin, Filangieri, Say, and so on. Pestel advised his associates to read Beccaria, Filangieri, Machiavelli, Voltaire, Helvetius, Adam Smith.[30]

The government of Nicholas I readily accepted the view that the Decembrist movement was a case of aping Europe, an imitative attempt to transplant Western notions. The Government emphasized the liaison with and borrowing from certain European secret societies and the mechanical influence of European impressions.[31] The historian of the movement, V. I. Semevski, agreed that 'the best university for many Decembrists was Western Europe'.[32] A more recent student, while admitting the role of local conditions, emphasizes the influence of the French Revolution on the origin and development of the Decembrist movement.[33]

An examination of the education and contacts of the future Decembrists reveals that the movement was not the automatic adoption of Western European impulses which the government claimed it was. The Russians at that time were not in a hurry in their visits to Europe. They had personal contacts with celebrities, attended lectures, studied educational and legal systems, constantly making notes in their diaries, Paul Krivtsov, with his brothers, studied in Switzerland in the same boarding-school with the sons of Robert Owen; he later studied law and political economy in

[30] M. V. Dovnar-Zapolski, *Ideals of the Decembrists,* Moscow, 1907, pp. 210-211.

[31] Cf. Sergei Hessen, *Decembrists before the Court of History, 1825-1925,* Leningrad, 1925.

[32] Semevski, *op. cit.,* p. 205.

[33] E. I. Tarasov, *The Decembrist Nikolia Ivanovitch Turgenev in the Epoch of Alexander I,* Samara, 1922, p. xii.

Berlin; in 1814 Benjamin Constant arranged a dinner in his honour in Geneva, and among the guests were Sismondi and Dumont, the translator of Bentham.[34]

The recognized head of the movement, P. I. Pestel, received his initial education in Dresden, N. I. and S. I. Muravyev-Apostol in Paris, and many of the others were educated by foreign teachers but in Russia. Pestel, when already a commissioned officer, took courses with Professor Hermann; Prince Th. Shakhovskoi, after entering the civil service in Moscow, took courses with Schlözer in the same way as Prince Valerian Golitsin; Alexander V. Muravyev studied with Professors Raupach and Hermann; Naryshkin with Professors Kunitsyn and Hermann; Brigan with Raupach; Ryleyev took private lessons in political economy with Professor Plisov.[35] In 1816 Pestel, S. and M. Muravyev-Apostol, Prince S. Trubetskoi, Prince Ilya Dolgorukov, F. N. Glinka, Nikita Muravyev, and the brothers Shipov took jointly a private course in political economy with Professor Hermann at his home, sharing the expenses of the instruction.[36] All of these teachers were persecuted by the government prior to 1825; all were admirers and followers of Smithianism. The written testimonies of the Decembrists at the trial all emphasize their interest in political economy and are crowded by the names of Adam Smith, Filangieri, Say. The four volumes of Adam Smith were sent to Sergei Krivtsov in his Siberian prison upon his special request.[37]

The predominance of English ideas can best be illustrated by the fact that the conspirators named among others Speranski, Mordvinov, and Kochubei as the heads of the future provisional government. In comparison with the other candidates, such as D. N. Senyavin, or General A. P. Yermolov, the above-mentioned three (all of them previously discussed in this chapter) have a pronounced colouring; they were the leaders of Smithianism in the Russia of Alexander I.[38] The government suspected that Arkadi

---

[34] Cf. M. Gershenson, *The Decembrist Krivtsov*, 2nd ed., Moscow-Berlin, 1923.

[35] Cf. Dovnar-Zapolski, *op. cit.*, pp. 223-224.

[36] Tarasov, *op. cit.*, p. 256.

[37] His brother Nicolas built a beautiful anglicized estate in Lyubichi, Saratov Government, where he lived with all the comfort and etiquette of the English gentry.

[38] Speranski and Mordvinov were appointed by Nicolas I to the Supreme Criminal Court in charge of the trial of the conspirators. The only vote against the death penalty was Mordvinov's. It was these two men's fate to pass judgment not only on friends and acquaintances but also on the leading Smithianist and collaborator of both: N. I. Turgenev. In his *La Russie et les Russes* Turgenev later denied any participation in the conspiracy. He spent most of his life in exile and died in 1871.

Al. Stolypin, Mordvinov's son-in-law and a friend of Speranski, also participated in the conspiracy.

In taking up English theories the Decembrists concentrated on and sharpened their political aspects. The draft of a constitution prepared by Nikita Muravyev even vividly reminds one, in some parts, of the United States' form of Government, and describes the future position of the Emperor as that of a 'supreme official of the Russian government'.[39]

Generally speaking, all the Decembrists insisted chiefly on political freedom and civil rights. Even in the question of serfdom they mostly limited themselves to demanding civil rights for everybody. The Decembrists advocated the emancipation of serfs without land grants. This was in line with the teachings of economic liberalism. Even Pestel at first stated that emancipation of serfs should not deprive the landlords of income. N. I. Turgenev differed in this matter from the other Decembrists as, without being absolutely consistent, he sometimes argued in favour of emancipation with land grants. Years later one of the less known Decembrists, M. S. Lunin, a cousin of the Muravyevs, an unusually colourful and strong personality, in a memoir written in Siberia sadly remarked: 'To undertake a political organization before the social basis is secured is equivalent to enlargement of an edifice lacking any foundation.'[40] Few of the conspirators made any concrete economic plans. The economic conditions of the period were not ripe for a revolution. In Pushkin's words,

> What is necessary for London
> Is premature for Moscow.

The only economic thinker in the leading group was P. I. Pestel. His *The Russian Truth*, an unfinished pamphlet intended as a guide for the future provisional government, was until recently the best and only source, though fragmentary, for information about the intentions of the most radical of the Decembrists.

As often happens in similar cases, parties and groups tried to make political capital of Pestel's ideas. Herzen called him a 'socialist prior to socialism'; an academic historian, M. M. Kovalevski, characterized Pestel's views as communism; Masaryk found a few socialist inclinations in Pestel's thought; V. Y. Zheleznov

[39] Of the six volumes of the *Alliance of Salvation* four were Muravyev's, the discussions of his draft constitution took place at Muravyev's house.

[40] M. S. Lunin, *Coup d'oeil sur les affaires de Poloneg*, Urik, 1840. Cf. S. I. Hessen and M. S. Kogan, *the Decembrist Lunin and His Time*, Leningrad, 1926.

stressed elements of the class struggle theory in *The Russian Truth;* and the Marxian historian M. Pokrovski claimed Pestel was a predecessor of the Russian Populists.

Pestel's recently discovered French manuscript *Practical Principles of Political Economy,*[41] written about 1820, gives us more insight into the theoretical background of the intellectual leader of the Decembrists.

S. Milman, the discoverer of the manuscript, qualifies Pestel at this period as the 'first ideologist of the petty bourgeoisie in Russia', basing this on Pestel's interest in Sismondi. But even he has to admit that it was not a case of a slavish imitation and that on the whole Pestel's conception is quite distinct from that of Sismondi. The following statement certainly does not sound Sismondi-like; 'A poorly organized industry leads to the worst consequences in all countries, and philosophical considerations regarding the nature of property and human rights are not appropriate in dealing with establishment of manufactures in the country.'[42]

It is true that Pestel's views underwent a certain evolution between the writing of *Practical Principles* and of *The Russian Truth.* The theory of economic liberalism remained intact, but in problems of economic policy Pestel became influenced more by concrete conditions than by abstract theories. One can feel in his numerous drafts of the *Principles* the steady pressure of actual conditions, the adjustment of his theories to the conflicts of Russian reality. In his early writings he even considered the introduction of guilds in order to assure quality of production. While his opinions in regard to the agrarian problem fluctuated, Pestel favoured governmental intervention and stated in *The Russian Truth* that the redistribution of land nationalized by the state was an essential part of civic rights.

As we can see, the influence of English liberalism was notable but not exclusive in the theory of the Decembrist movement. The movement was more political than social and economic in character; it did not have a crystallized economic programme, but in the choice of the future leaders of the country the Decembrists openly manifested their adherence to English ideas and ideals.

This foreign character of their liberalism was emphasized by Herzen, who rather overstressed the Russian conspirators' lack of popular support. It is true that they did not have mass support, but they certainly represented the intellectual youth of the cultured part of the upper classes of that period.

English economic liberalism did not have any foundation, any

[41] *The Red Archive,* Vol. XIII, 1925, pp. 174-249.
[42] *Ibid,* p. 185.

*raison d'être,* any roots in the Russian environment. Russia was not ripe for it; capitalism was just in *statu nascendi,* and the slowly growing Russian genuine bourgeoisie wanted protection, not free trade, and expected government intervention in its favour. Consequently liberalism did not have any appeal and could not find any support in Russian society.

The English influence was also weak in the academic study of economics in Russia. Infatuation with Adam Smith was, as we have seen, a short-lived episode, and this current of thought was followed by few Russian professors in the first thirty years of the 19th century. Moscow was the first centre of social studies in Russia; and while Adam Smith, as we have seen, made his first appearance in Moscow, St. Petersburg was the chief propagandist of Smithian teachings.

After the brief period of official intoxication with English liberalism we find Adam Smith's name mentioned from time to time in university catalogues. N. T. Butyrski announced a course at the University of St. Petersburg, entitled 'Political Economy and the Science of Finances According to the Theory of Adam Smith'. His formal speech at the university in 1829 dealt with 'The Study of Adam Smith and the Moral Current Which Should Be Applied to Political Economy'. In the catalogue for 1830 we find A. J. Nikitenko offering 'The Theory of National Wealth According to Adam Smith'. in 1859 one of N. Ch. Bunge's students, Professor G. M. Zechanovetzki, published a thesis on *The Importance of Adam Smith for Political Economy.* It was not a revival of interest in Adam Smith but just one in a series of dissertations prepared by Bunge's students and associates (e.g., T. Sidorenko's on Turgot in 1858 or A. Geisman's on the physiocrats in 1847). Other English classical economists were relatively unknown in Russia with the exception of Malthus, who in 1830 was elected an honorary member of the University of St. Petersburg.

The individualist liberalism of the British classical school never became a dominant or even an influential trend in old Russia. The horrors of England's early industrialization impressed Russian thought. Pushkin expressed the common feeling in this, as in many other instances, in his *Village, Notes on Radishchev,* and, especially, *Conversation with an Englishman Concerning Russian Peasants,* where the Englishman insists that 'a free Englishman lives in a greater misery than a Russian slave' and reports the complaints of English factory workers. Typically he stressed unemployment as a result of mechanization.[43]

---

[43] In his *Considerations on the Building of Railroads,* while giving the

33

C

The influence of Ricardo in Russia was negligible, though he was occasionally studied by Russian economists. For instance, he was reviewed and criticized by Professor V. S. Poroshin of St. Petersburg; I. E. Yanson's thesis dealt with Ricardo's rent theory.

The liberal period of Alexander II was more influenced by French Utopians, as we shall see in the next chapter, but John Stuart Mill had some prominence, if not influence, in academic teachings. A thesis was defended at the University of St Petersburg in 1867 by N. Rozhdestvenski *On the Role of John Stuart Mill among Contemporary Economists,* and N. I. Ziber at Kiev in the early seventies discussed Ricardo as a bridge to Karl Marx (see Chapter IV).

But generally speaking, the free trade theory together with admiration of Western industrialization and credit organization had at that time a distinctly French accent. The periodicals of St. Petersburg, especially the *Economic Indicator* published by Professor Vernadski, *Fatherland Notes,* and *The Voice,* clearly indicated this French influence. They were fighting with Moscow's protectionism of the period represented by the *Messenger of Industry.* Only few of the mid-19th-century Russian economists—among them Butovski in St. Petersburg, Stepanov in Kharkov, Chivilev in Moscow, Gorlov in Kazan (later in Moscow), Ivan K. Babst in Kazan (also later in Moscow; a most talented but neglected Russian economist), to some degree N. Ch. Bunge in Kiev (later the minister of finance) and V. P. Bezobrazov—could be classified as adherents of the Manchester school. The conditions of life in Russia were in conflict with classical theories, which in their abstractness and individualist severity were strange and unacceptable to the ethical spirit of the Russian intelligentsia.

The neoclassical line received some attention and acquired a few followers at the end of the 19th and beginning of the 20th century. There were several who took up the Austrian brand of neoclassicism, like W. F. Zaleski and R. M. Orzhentski; the latter definitely showed the influence of Alfred Marshall. The mathematical trend made its appearance in Russia in works by V. K. Dmitriev and N. N. Shaposhnikov, and was fostered by the great Russian statistician A. A. Chuprov and his school. But as a rule the English and English-dyed brand of economics did not appeal to Russian taste. Only the University of St. Vladimir at Kiev became and remained a fortress of laissez faire, combining individualist liberalism in

---

usual emphasis to difficulties (especially snow removal), Pushkin insisted that the railroads were a matter for private individuals; the government should have nothing to do with it.

economics and a strong political nationalism. With few exceptions (for example, N. Ch. Bunge) this school took a conservative stand in questions of economic policy. But there were few exceptions even in Kiev, where one found Marxists like Ziber, V Y. Zheleznov, and M. V. Bernatski, and where the influential N. Ch. Bunge presented a Russian version of *Kathedersozialismus*.

There were liberalist-inclined economists in other universities: in St Petersburg, for instance, Vreden, Georgievski, Chodski, whose teachings also show a moderate historism. But this group was not popular with the Russian youth; they failed to find an echo in the minds and conscience of the Russian intelligentsia, which was creating its own theories and theorists.

Bezobrazov was correct in stating that 'The "paradoxes" of Adam Smith were an exceptional phenomenon in the history of our public economy, just as were the legislative measures inspired by Catherine II at the end of the eighteenth century under the influence of certain French physiocrats of Quesnay's school'.

# III. French Influence

Monsieur Beaupré, the tutor of young Grinev, who was ordered to be sent from Moscow together with a yearly supply of wine and olive oil, in his own fatherland was a barber; later, in Prussia, a soldier; later went to Russia " pour être ouchitel". [to be a teacher].

PUSHKIN, *The Captain's Daughter*.

W H I L E the English influence on economic thought in Russia was hardly more than an isolated early episode, the French influence took place in two episodes: the short-lived physiocratic interest of Catherine II, and the strong admiration and reception of French Utopian socialist theories in the forties followed by the penetration of an enterprising Saint-Simonist spirit in the late fifties and sixties of the 19th century.

Surprisingly enough for an agricultural country, there were no physiocratic theorists in Russia, though some of the general ideas aroused a weak echo during the first half of the reign of Catherine II. The establishment of the Imperial Free Economic Society in St. Petersburg in 1766,[44] the famous *Instruction,* and the Manifesto of 1786 regarding the establishment of the State Loan Bank developed evident sympathies in this direction.

A reaction against mercantilist regimentation is presented most strongly in the *Instruction*. 'Commerce', one of its well-known statements declares, 'withdraws from where it is being handicapped, and settles where its peace is not disturbed.'

---

[44] The Empress gave to the society immediately after its formation a sum of money to be awarded as a prize for the best essay upon "The Relative Advantage of Private and Public Ownership of Land." A year after the prize was announced, one hundred and sixty-two essays had been received, the competitors representing nearly every country in Europe. The essays were of "enormous length" and were written in French, Latin, Dutch, Swedish, Russian, and so forth. The Russian authors were generally in favour of public ownership, the foreign writers generally in favour of private ownership. The prize was awarded to Beardé de l'Abbaye, Doctor of Law, of Aix-la-Chapelle. His paper contained a systematic treatment of the peasant question and, on the whole, reflected the influence of the physiocrats. The magnificent library of the society contained collections of the materials of local governmental and economic history. Cf. A. E. Khodnev, *History of the Imperial Free Economic Society, 1765-1865,* St. Petersburg, 1865. Also James Mavor, *An Economic History of Russia,* London, 1914, Vol. I, pp. 312-313.

In conventional physiocratic style Catherine II declares in the *Instruction* that 'agriculture is the first and main occupation which must be stimulated'.

The *Instruction* clearly recognized the growing differentiation of population and the formation of urban classes. We read in it: 'Commoners inhabit the towns and exercise handicraft, commerce, arts, and sciences. This group of population, from which the state expects substantial benefit if it is based strictly on virtue and its diligence is being fostered, is the middle one. It enjoys liberty and is not included either in the nobility or in the class of soil tillers.'

This leitmotiv of freedom of enterprise was frequently repeated in various governmental ukases. For instance in one of Nevember 27, 1767, Catherine said about a deteriorating state leather factory: 'When this factory is not in state hands, then, I assume, there will be enough leather. The monopoly of this state factory was harmful for the people and the state profit has not compensated for the damage.'

In a letter to Diderot summarizing the debate in the commission working on the *Instruction,* Catherine stated that in this commission 'all three classes of population shake the air with their loud words in defence of their interests; the agriculturist appeals to property rights, the merchant to the rights of freedom, and the people to the rights of humanity'.

Diderot and Mercier de la Rivière visited St. Petersburg on the Empress' invitation (Diderot in the capacity of 'Ambassador and Minister Plenipotentiary of the Encyclopedic Republic', as Prince Peter Vyazemski phrased the invitation), but Catherine in a letter to Voltaire complained that Diderot regarded the Russians as quadrupeds and kindly agreed to take care of putting them on their 'hind legs'.

The Empress did not support Diderot's plan for establishing a university or school of public instruction in sciences and liberal arts; she obviously resented his criticism and mentorial guidance. And Diderot on his part was not misled by the visible culture and progressiveness of Catherine's court. He called St. Petersburg a 'city of palaces surrounded by desert lots'.

Diderot told the Russians that 'not only palaces are necessary'; there have to be streets—series of private homes for the industrial population which would link together the various 'palaces'.

The French Revolution ended Catherine's flirtation with the fashionable intellectual imports from Paris. Pushkin was probably too severe in his statement that history 'will disclose the important errors of her political economy, the cheapness of her legislation, her disgraceful buffoonery in relations with the philosophers of her century'.[45]

The Napoleonic Wars and the Anglomania of Alexander I's period abolished any remaining traces of formal French influence in Russian economic thought.

The government now persecuted the admirers of the French Revolution. The case of A. N. Radishchev is typical. His *Journey from St. Petersburg to Moscow,* composed in a form borrowed from Sterne, was one of the first violent and eloquent castigations of the administration and of conditions in Russia. It demanded equality of rights, including, of course, emancipation of the serfs, and predicted, failing this, a revolt of the masses. Radishchev was arrested by order of Catherine II, tried, and sentenced to death; the sentence was then commuted to exile in Siberia.

The war of 1812 caused a strong surge of national consciousness and anti-French feeling in the Russian intelligentsia. It resulted in a negative attitude toward the French philosophers.

The popular satire of this period, *Insane Asylum* by Voyeikov, was rich in ridicule of the French philosophers, especially Diderot.

Pushkin's *Roslavlev* (1831) gives a striking picture of the anti-French movement of 1812: 'Salons became full of patriots. . . . Some of them emptied their snuffboxes of French tobacco and snuffed Russian; others burned a dozen of French pamphlets; some gave up *lafitte* [wine] and turned to sour *shchi* [cabbage soup].'

A reaction against the Francophobia of 1812 was caused by personal contacts: Russian residents in Paris and French emigrants in Russia. The French refugees, of course, agitated against the French Revolution, but at the same time they spread the influence of French culture and literature. Typically, the brother of Marat, whose name was changed by Catherine II into de Boudry, was teaching French literature in the Alexandrovski Lyceum.

Even after 1815 the ideas of the French Revolution were astir all over Europe. Soon they began to win ground.

While the Decembrist movement, in my opinion, was influenced most by English economic and political thought, its organizational forms were of a continental European character and, as we have seen, showed some dependence on French contacts. The Young Italy and Young Germany movements found a parallel in a kind of Young Russia movement in the thirties. The period of Nicholas I was, in Herzen's words, a 'remarkable time of outward slavery and inner emancipation'.

A timid awakening of Russian thought suppressed by the re-

45 *Historical Notes,* No. 1 (1822).

action began after 1830. The breaking of the ice started in Moscow. There were special reasons for Moscow's pre-eminence in this intellectual revival. Moscow's society was always more independent, as it contained wealthy nobility not in service of the state; Moscow was free from the court's pressure; Moscow was, more than St. Petersburg, the cradle of all the 'circles' and societies so numerous in old Russia, and it still cherished the memory of the Friendly Scientific Society formed in the eighties of the 18th century by Novikov, Schwartz, and Lopukhin, which was the origin and centre of the intelligentsia of Moscow.

It is difficult to visualize now the role of the Moscow University in that time. E. H. Carr describes it in the following words:

'While Moscow had arisen with renewed splendour and prestige from the ashes of the Napoleonic conflagration, the Decembrist insurrection had made Petersburg the citadel of reaction. Advanced thought transferred its headquarters to Moscow, where youth could still breathe and think with some slight vestige of freedom. The University of Moscow became a hive of intellectual activity. Students formed themselves into groups or, in the terminology of the day, 'circles', which soon extended their influences beyond the confines of the university itself, and created, in philosophy, in literature, and in politics, a new school of Russian thought. Two of these 'circles' achieved eminence and are remembered. The first, to which Alexander Herzen and his friend Ogarev belonged, applied itself to politics and found its spiritual home among the early French socialists. The second, which came to be known as 'the circle of Stankevich', eschewed politics and sought the truth, less dangerously though not less daringly, in the pages of German poets and philosophers.'[46]

In the field of economic ideas the revival developed in two directions: idealism influenced by German philosophy, and Utopianism infatuated with French socialism.

Of the university groups in Moscow, one influenced by the new French socialism was led by Herzen and Ogarev; the other, deeply involved in the German philosophy of Schelling, Fichte, and Hegel, led by Stankevich, counted among its members Botkin, Belinski, Granovski, and later K. Aksakov and Samarin, Katkov, Kudryavtsev, Kavelin. There was no intellectual love lost between the two groups; they called each other respectively '*frondeurs* and Frenchmen' and 'sentimentalists and Germans'. By a turn in the forties the '*frondeurs* and Frenchmen' became the Westerners, and the 'senti-

---

[46] E. H. Carr, *Michael Bakunin*, London, 1937, p. 30.

THE SPIRIT OF RUSSIAN ECONOMICS

mentalists and Germans' joined the Slavophiles under the intellectual leadership of Khomyakov and Kireyevski.

Especially between the two revolutions of 1830 and 1848 French Utopian socialism ('The poisonous honey brought from France', as Tennyson called it) spread with unusual rapidity all over the world. No country, no nation was immune. Numerous community experiments in the United States were based on all kinds of imitations of variously coloured French socialist systems. A similar development took place in Russia. But while in the United States the protagonists jumped into an immediate application of the French ideas in their communities, the Russians speculated on the reorganization of the entire world (including Russia, of course) along these lines. It was a case of Russian *pensemos en grande,* to use the Spanish expression.

While in the United States almost every brand of French Utopian socialist doctrine found admirers and experimentalists, in Russia Fourierism and Saint-Simonism dominated the field. The Russian intelligentsia studied the political aspects, emphasizing the social factor, but left it to practical men to make sometimes unexpected conclusions and transform their ideas into actuality. The irony of history is interesting: In the realistic world of the United States, Utopian socialism, practically applied, resulted in the establishment of radically conceived communities; in idealistic Russia it led, as we shall see, to formations of modern capitalism—spread of industrial enterprises, development of transportation, organization of banking, etc.

We shall follow in the next chapter the thought and fate of the sentimentalists and Germans', acquainting ourselves now with the '*frondeurs* and Frenchmen'. In the twenties of the 19th century the Western intellectual magnet for Russian youth was the University of Göttingen; the idealists of the thirties started peregrinations to Berlin; the forties showed a gravitation toward Paris, to 'the country of Saint-Simon, Cabet, and Fourier'.

The first nucleus of a Russian Saint-Simonist circle was formed early in the thirties at the University of Moscow by Herzen, N. Sazonov, and I. M. Satin.

Annenkov recalls in his memoirs how the group *at that time* gave more attention to social rather than to philosophical problems, and worshipped Saint-Simon, not Hegel. Herzen, a young student of the faculty of natural sciences and mathematics, headed this group[47]. In Annenkov's words, 'Herzen ran around with his Saint-Simon as if with the Koran'.

[47] *Literary Reminiscences,* Academia edition, Leningrad, 1928, p. 329.

Soon they began to develop ambitious plans such as one in 1834 for the publication of an encyclopedical journal[48]. In the same year they were arrested by the police.

Based on circumstantial evidence regarding their 'way of thought' Herzen, together with Ogarev anl Sokolovski, was accused of participation in a 'conspiracy, prevented by the arrest of young men devoted to the doctrine of Saint-Simonism'.

But the movement was making progress. Annenkov recalls in the already quoted memoirs that when he returned in 1843 from abroad to St. Petersburg he found there a 'reflection of many phases of the intellectual life of Paris'. Works by Proudhon, Cabet, Fourier 'were in everybody's hands', were the object of passionate discussions, and caused 'problems and expectations of all kinds'. And Saltykov-Shchedrin wrote: 'From the France of Saint-Simon, Cabet, Fourier, Louis Blanc, and especially of George Sand, belief in mankind was penetrating Russia; from France we received the assurance that the golden age is before and not behind us'.

There were not at that time, as far as I know, any Russian translations of the French writers; but the small groups of interested people belonged mostly to the nobility, who knew French. These ideas soon penetrated larger groups of Russian society. Herzen testified that in the forties the university youth as well as students in the lyceum of Tsarskoye Selo were following the 'realistic, i.e. positive-scientific current'.

To this period belong two forgotten Russian economists, V. A. Milyutin and V. N. Maikov. Milyutin, who as a young student in 1845-46 attended Petrashevski's meetings, became professor at the University of St. Petersburg but committed suicide in 1855 at the age of twenty-nine. He energetically denied all laissez-faire theories, stating that the teachings of the 'economists' (as he called the followers of Adam Smith in contrast to socialists) did not satisfy the contemporary requirements of life and science. Only socialist theories were, in his view, permeated by the new spirit, and their aim was to find the ideal social organization. Sismondi was for Milyutin the bridge between 'economists' and socialists.

Maikov, a professional publicist, preached a theory of profit-sharing (dolshchina), demanding a just division of the profit between owner and workers. Even in his early student publication

---

Ogarev in his poems described this group as children of the Decembrists and apostles of the new world, disciples of Fourier and Saint-Simon. See especially his poem *Radaev*.

[48] In later years N. P. Ogarev worked on a plan for a popular poly-technical school.

*On the Relation between Production and Distribution of Wealth* he developed his theory, considering it the main theme of the argument started by Smith and Sismondi.

We have discussed already the tradition of secret societies and circles in Russia. The first half of the 19th century witnessed all kinds of them: literary, like the famous groups of Pushkin's period; political, like the Decembrists; and many others, that camouflaged their real interest, like the numerous societies started by Prince Odoyevski. These societies bloomed most luxuriantly in the twenties and thirties of the 19th century. They were devoted mostly to problems of aesthetics, literature and philosophy. The aristocratic salons of Princess Zinaida Volkonski, of A. Elagina, of Prince V. F. Odoyevski, and of Count Sollogub deserve a place of honour in the history of Russian culture. Problems of literature prevailed in the well-known *Arzamas* and in the gatherings at Nestor Kukolnik's, as well as in the less aristocratic circles of Veltman and Glinka. These Russian societies and circles were a clear case of escapism. Belinski emphasized this element: 'We are in quarrel with reality . . . where is our haven? On an uninhabited island which is our circle'.

In the forties and the fifties the character of the circles and societies changed: a decline of aesthetic and literary interests occurred parallel to a shift in membership. A transition took place from aristocratic salons to circles of 'men of various ranks' *(rasnochintzy)* in which many representatives of the nobility still participated.

From the forties up to the Soviet Revolution, Russia witnessed series of secret groups, circles, and societies in whose discussions politics and social questions dominated. But while in the first half of the 19th century they were usually *conspiracies of ideas*, the second half of the century saw a growth of *conspiracies of action*. One such secret organization with a new type of membership, but still distinctly a conspiracy of ideas, was the famous Petrashevski group, a Russian echo of the 1848 movement in Europe.

It seems that Professor V. S. Poroshin had a large influence on Petrashevski. (V. Maikov was also a student of Poroshin.) Poroshin himself was a peculiar figure. It is interesting to read in Grigoryev's work on the University of St. Petersburg[49] that "Poroshin succeeded Butyrski, who never mentioned even the existence of a socialist school of political economy. Poroshin's lectures appeared especially profound to the students, and quite soon—due to his versatile

[49] V. V. Grigoryev, *Historical Notes on the Imperial University of St. Petersburg*, St. Petersburg, 1870, p. 168.

knowledge, humanitarian tendencies, and nobility of character—
Poroshin became one of the most popular professors of the university, in spite of an absolute lack of eloquence'[50].

The membership of Petrashevski's group was not as aristocratic as the Decembrists'; there were more from the middle class; it was a 'movement of *rasnochintzy*'. It included future great writers like Dostoyevski and Saltykov, professors like the young Milyutin, government officials (among them the later famous Danilevski), officers, students, merchants, and 'petty bourgeois including tobacconists', as the police agent Liprandi described it in his report.

Their ideas were of more or less Fourierist character. I. L. Yastrzhembski, who addressed the group at some of their Friday meetings on problems of political economy wrote in his memoirs: 'All young people of my acquaintance as well as myself were so occupied with the social-economic movement started in Europe that we almost neglected events in Russia and St. Petersburg'.[51]

While the emphasis in the Decembrist movement had been on political reforms and the method preached was a political revolution, the Petrashevski group dreamed of a social revolution. Their ties were closer with Western Europe than with the Decembrists. A member of the group, Akhsharumov, aptly remarked that instead of 'Petrashevtzi' they should be labelled 'Russian socialists'.

The fate of Petrashevski and his group was tragic. In December, 1849, on the Semenovski Place in St. Petersburg they were standing blindfolded on the scaffold when the Emperor's commutation of sentence arrived[52]. The reader remembers, of course, the pathetic description of these minutes in Dostoyevski's *Idiot*. The Petrashevski group was in close contact with the Alexandrovski Lyceum of Tsarskoe Selo. This famous exclusive institution, immortalized by Pushkin, was the *alma mater* of many Decembrists. Petrashevski was its alumnus, as were several other members of his circle. In the forties the interests of the lyceum's students were drawn more especially to the teachings of Saint-Simon. E. I. Lamanski (also a member of the circle) recalled in his memoirs how he and his colleagues—the future statesmen of Russia—Count Reutern, Greig, Bezobrazov, and others were influenced by the

---

[50] After twelve years of teaching at the university (1835-1847) Poroshin moved to Paris, where he continued his studies, writing on Russian problems and engaging in a polemical battle with Garnier published in the *Journal des Economistes*.

[51] I. L. Yastrzhembski " Memoirs of a Petrashevetz," *Past Years*, 1906, No. 1, p. 21.

[52] Yastrzhembski's punishment was four years of hard labour, increased by Tsar Nicholas to six years. Later he taught at the Technological Institute in St. Petersburg.

fascinating presentation of contemporary currents in political economy by Professor Ivanovski, who was abroad on a scientific mission during the thirties.[53]

The Alexandrovski Lyceum was one of the centres of the movement; it later became the bridge between Saint-Simonist theories and practical endeavour. The pride of Russian aristocratic youth formed this group of young dreamers, later statesmen, bureaucrats, and leaders. Possibly the aristocratic origin of Saint-Simon, soldier and businessman who claimed to be of royal blood, the disciple of D'Alembert, impressed his Russian followers. While Saint-Simon constructed grandiose schemes of a better future world, his programme of industrialization was in tune with the needs and demands of the Russian economy. 'The golden age is before us'— this statement of Saint-Simon excited the Russian youth. While his doctrine was discussed and debated by the younger generation, his practical programme was enthusiastically applied by the next generation.

Another memoir relates that V. P. Bezobrazov began at that time to study the theories of the newer economists, that he was influenced by the events of 1848, and that a group of friends met weekly at Bezobrazov's.[54]

Lamanski revealed the intellectual idol of the group—the social theories of Saint-Simonism. Writings by the brothers Pereira, Michel Chevalier, and others were eagerly devoured.[55] Bezobrazov was the centre and the organizer of the movement.

The Saint-Simonist influence in Russia was much stronger than Fourierism especially because of its practical application in France, and it became popular in this form during the late forties and fifties when the discussion of liberal reforms was under way.

The rapidly developing periodical economic literature in the Russia of that time was full of echoes of the practical activity of the French Saint-Simonists. The Russian disciples believed that a way had been discovered for world reconstruction, that a new period of human history was dawning.

Official periodicals discussed the practical programme of Saint-Simonism in the same way as when, at the beginning of the century, their interest had concentrated on Adam Smith. Typically, in the journal of the Ministry of State Domains we find an elaborate

[53] " From the Memoirs of E. I. Lamanski," *Russian Antiquity*, January, 1915, p. 74.

[54] " To the Memory of V. P. Bezobrazov," *Russian Archive*, 1889, No. 12, p. 502.

[55] Lamanski, *op. cit.*, p. 75.

study by V. P. Bezobrazov entitled 'Crédit Mobilier'.[56] Its author
was aware of the especially attractive Saint-Simonist background
of the French bank. In this study, which discloses Bezobrazov's
solid knowledge of Pereira's speeches and of Crédit Mobilier
reports, he stated: 'A thought underlies the fundamentals of the
Crédit Mobilier which cannot leave one indifferent; in this thought
are preserved traces of the inspiration in early years of the chief
founders of the corporation—Isaac and Emile Pereira'. Reiterating
this very often, Bezobrazov emphasized his own sympathy for the
ideas of the Crédit Mobilier, in which he saw 'public welfare' and
'development of social industry', and an 'association of competing
economic elements'.[57]

The political emigrant N. Ogarev in Herzen's revolutionary *Bell*,
developing an elaborate programme in the economic field, also
favoured the banking projects of the period, combining Saint-
Simonist hierarchical organization of credit with the Russian *mir*
and expecting that capital investment through the bank would help
the village community to abolish individual land ownership.[58]

The future minister of finance Professor N. Ch. Bunge published
at that time his *Speech on Credit and Theory of Credit;* another
professor, I. K. Babst, spoke of the 'gigantic credit establishments
which are at prevent controlling and directing world industry'.
L. von Tengoborski studied the Crédit Mobilier, as did Y. A.
Gagemeister and Professor I. Vernadski; many *dei minores* published discussions on the same subject, and of course the group of
the lyceum—Bezobrazov, Lamanski, Terner, Nebolsin, and others
—was active. Members of the Imperial Free Economic Society
were labouring on the formation of 'an association for fostering
industrial possibilities', imitating Enfantin's attempts in Paris.

Michel Chevalier, the Saint-Simonist, collaborated in the first
issue of the *Economic Indicator* (1857), published by Professor
I. V. Vernadski. Vernadski introduced Chevalier as one of the
'famous contemporary economists'. If we browse through the
yellow pages of the few available copies of the *Messenger of
Industry* or the *Journal for Stockholders*, we witness everywhere
the same tendency which was aptly characterized by Professor S.
Pachman of the University of Kharkov as 'an imitation of the
French example in emphasis on public welfare and interest in the
formation of joint stock enterprise'.[59]

---

[56]V. P. Bezobrazov, " Crédit Mobilier," *Journal of the Ministry of State
Domains,* 1856, p. 85.
[57]*Ibid*, pp. 94, 329, 332.
[58] *Bell,* No. 89 (January 16, 1869), p. 78.
[59] S. Pachman, *On the Aims of the Intended Reform of Corporation*

There was a lively personal intercourse between the Russian and French Saint-Simonists, easily explained by the constant peregrinations of Russians to Paris. We know that some of the Decembrists occasionally met Saint-Simon himself. This was, for instance, the case with Lunin, whose sudden departure to Russia chagrined Saint-Simon, who felt that 'Russia was a fruitful ground for his teachings'.[60] It is not commonly known that Enfantin was personally acquainted with Russia: he sold wine in St. Petersburg in the twenties.

But in the fifties and sixties when the former 'Lyceists' appeared in responsible positions on the public stage, they came in contact with the practical followers of the French Saint-Simonists. The leaders of the movement, Emile and Isaac Pereira, were frequent visitors in St. Petersburg; newspapers announced their arrivals in advance. Michel Chevalier and de Molinari were fêted by Russian economists, and contributed to Russian periodicals. Chevalier was elected honorary member of the University of St. Petersburg in 1869. The journal *Le Nord,* started with the co-operation of Russians in Paris, was represented in St. Petersburg by F. G. Terner; subscriptions to the *Economic Journal* were solicited in Paris, and reports from Paris filled the pages of Russian economic periodicals.

Ferdinand de Lesseps was in correspondence with Russian leaders of the period; in a letter to the editor of the *Journal d'Odessa* he solicited subscriptions to shares in the Suez Canal Company.

The famous contractor Kokorev, one of the richest men of the period, representative of the national merchant class, complained that 'on Russian soil, during the coronation of Alexander II, appeared from Paris the notorious 'affairist' of Napoleon III, Pereira, with a gang of bakers, barbers, shoemakers, and so on, who called themselves "expert engineers" '. His complaint was understandable: the General Company of Russian Railways founded by the Pereiras was the bridge to the Crédit Mobilier, to the ideas of practical Saint-Simonism, to growing industrialization and the penetration of foreign capital. It was another aspect of the perpetual antagonism between Moscow and St. Petersburg.

In another study many years ago I had the occasion to discuss this relationship[61]. I believe it proved for Russia the interrelationship between Saint-Simonist visions of the coming industrial order

*Legislation,* Kharkov, 1861, p. 7.
[60] Cf. S. I. Hessen and M. S. Kogan, *The Decembrist Lunin and His Time,* Leningrad, 1926, p. 53.
[61] *Commercial Banks in Russia,* Vol. I, History, Petrograd, 1918.

and the formation of the credit organization—a relationship emphasized for France by Johannes Plenge, for Germany by Lotz and Model-Loeb, and for Austria by Fritz Steiner. Later on I discovered the same relationship in far-off Brazil, where the birth of modern industrialism also took place under disciples of Saint-Simon and with the collaboration of his followers in the business world[62].

The idealist part of Saint-Simonism soon evaporated in Russia. As in France and in other parts of the world, the disciples succeeded in opening the road to new economic forms; they were the pioneers of credit and means of communication; but the disciples destroyed the master.

In the Russia of the sixties V. P. Bezobrazov was the leader in theoretical studies and organizer of the discussions. His friend E. I. Lamanski, son of the director of the Bureau of Credit, later himself director of the State Bank, was also active. With them were the future minister of finance Count M. Ch. Reutern; his assistant, G. P. Nebolsin; the director of the Bureau of Credit, Y. A. Gagemeister; F. G. Terner, and others. Professor I. V. Vernadski joined them, N. Ch. Bunge sympathized, and I. K. Babst agreed on many points.

Their private discussions were followed in St. Petersburg by public conferences like those of their French *confrères*. Imitating the French, they formed a Political Economic Committee of the Statistical Committee of the Imperial Russian Geographical Society. The list of founders is almost identical with the roster of the followers of French Saint-Simonism. A parallel committee of the Imperial Free Economic Society presented the same picture.

This group had a strong influence on Russian administration during the 'Epoch of Great Reforms' of the sixties. The conservative merchant class called them *Oni* ('They') and accused them of being dreamers ignorant of Russia's actual life and needs.

The famous 'economic dinners' of this period were a kind of continuation of the secret societies of the younger generation; they began in the early sixties, organized by the same leaders, mostly former students of the Alexandrovski Lyceum: Bezobrazov, Lamanski, Greig, Terner, and others. The economic dinners lasted in this form for about thirty-five years. The conservative *Moscow Reports* called Bezobrazov's dinners the 'ancestor of all our dinner-parliaments and other talking places'. This rather exclusive organization degenerated later into a kind of bureaucratic institution, and

[62] *Brazil: A Study of Economic Types*, University of North Carolina Press, 1935.

another group, formed in the eighties, which first gathered in the home of A. P. Subbotin (the editor of the *Economic Journal*), took more formal shape after 1887, and was legalized in 1890 as the Association of Economists[63]. The Bezobrazov dinners took place at the restaurant Donon; among the participants bureaucrats and financiers predominated, mostly free-traders. Subbotin's dinners took place for some time at the restaurant Contant; its participants were mostly manufacturers and representatives of professional groups.

One of the most active and interesting personalities of this period, Bezobrazov, bitterly lamented in his memoirs the intellectual degeneration of his group.

The economic background of this penetration by French Saint-Simonism is clear. While its Utopian and quasi-socialist features appealed to the Russian ethical socialists, the practical programme of Saint-Simonism, which called for industrialization, was the answer to Russian needs developing in that period.

It was the beginning of urbanization, pressure for railroads and other means of communications, for organization of credit, for new form of industry. 'Associations' in the form of large stock companies and, especially, the Saint-Simonist idea of the magic role of credit were tempting in a country of large potentialities and small accumulation of capital in the first stage of its industrialization process.

---

[63] As a young student I delivered two papers before this association, prior to World War I.

# IV. German Influence

Vladimir Lensky, handsome, youthful,
Whose soul was shaped in Göttingen
From misty Germany, Vladimir
Had brought the fruits of learned tree.
>           PUSHKIN, *Eugene Onegin*

How from our earliest times we learned
to think
Without the Germans no salvation!
>           GRIBOYEDOV. *Woe from Wit*

W H I L E the English and French influence on the formation
of Russian economic thought resulted in some more or less
intense episodes, the German influence has been a lasting and
strong one. There are many causes explaining this influence
stimulated by geographical proximity, economic relations, and
personal contacts.

Germans played a substantial role in the internal organization
of the Russian Empire. Russian people used to call almost every
foreigner *Nemetz*.[64] The part of the old city of Moscow inhabited
by foreigners was called 'the German suburb' (*Nemetzkaya
Sloboda*). The Imperial Academy of Sciences in St. Petersburg was
established in 1724 according to Leibnitz' plan, and until 1733
there was not a single Russian among the members. In its make-up
between 1725 and 1742 there were, according to Wilhelm von
Stieda, of forty-nine academicians five Swiss, five French, three
from the Baltic provinces, one Russian, and thirty-five Germans.[65]
'Various branches of science and learning were . . . planted on
Russian soil by German scholars: the great mathematician Euler
assisted in the foundation of a Russian mathematical school; the
famous historian Schlözer contributed to the formation of Russian
historical studies; somewhat later and at different times Weier-
strass, Bunsen, Liebig, Ritter, Grimm, Savigny, Ranke, Droysen,
and Mommsen, besides many others, trained Russian students in

---

64 The Latin-speaking foreigners were called " Franks " *(Friasi),* but the
common people did not make this distinction.

65 Wilhelm von Stieda, *"Die Anfänge der Kaiserlichen Akademie der
Wissenschaften,"* in *Jahrbücher für Kultur und Geschichte der Slaven,* N.F.,
B II, H. 1, Breslau, 1926, p. 137.

mathematics, chemistry, linguistics and folklore, and history.'[66]
In the field of social sciences the first university chairs of history,
economics, and statistics were occupied by Germans. Grellmann,
Heym, Kraft, von Schlözer (son), Hermann, Storch were among
the first Russian academic economists and statisticians; Bayer, G.
F. Müller, von Schlözer (father), Backmeister, Büsching, among the
first Russian academic historians.

Russia continuously imported German scholars during the 19th
century and sent her own youth to study in Germany. This inter-
change was especially strong in the field of economic studies in the
first thirty years of the 19th century.

German economists and statisticians were at that time imported
by the Russian government not only to organize education but also
to assist in organizing the administration of the country. Russian
contacts with English economists were incidental, sometimes by
way of correspondence only; there were not any English economists
residing, learning, and teaching in Russia. It happened that Thomas
Tooke, author of the famous *History of Prices*[67] was born in St.
Petersburg (1774), but this did not cause any interest on his part
in things Russian. French contacts were more frequent but of
rather ephemeral nature; the Encyclopedists and Saint-Simonists
were visitors to and not residents in Russia; they observed and
studied Russia from their hotel room windows.

German economists as a rule became settled, and adjusted
themselves in the new milieu or at least became interested in it;
they were residents and not visitors, they learned the language of
the country (the elder Schlözer was one of the first to decide to
learn Russian, and he spoke it), they participated in its life, they
became sometimes more conforming 'patriots' than the Russian
intelligentsia.

In the seventies and eighties of the 19th century the future cream
of German economists was making its first appearance in the
Russian Baltic provinces: Adolph Wagner, Karl Bücher, Wilhelm
von Stieda, Wilhelm Lexis, Karl Dietzel, to name just a few of the
more famous. The University of Dorpat, founded in 1802, was the
back door for penetration by German economists, as the Baltic
provinces were, generally speaking, the bridge from Germany and
the easiest road for the infiltration of German ideas. A. Brückner
was correct in emphasizing that 'with the conquest of the Baltic

[66] A. S. Lappo-Danilevski, "Science and Learning in Russia" in *Russian
Realities and Problems*, edited by J. D. Duff, Cambridge, England, 1917,
pp. 166-167.
[67] Thomas Tooke, *History of Prices*, London, 1838-1857.

provinces Russia had obtained not only some square miles of territory and a coast line immensely important for communications with Europe, but also spiritual capital in the form of German population; and the high interest on this capital became exceedingly profitable to the entire community'.[68]

Isolated missions of Russian students and scholars to Germany were frequent in the 18th century. Thus we know that Lomonosov was sent in 1736 to study under Christian Wolff in Marburg; we know that Radishchev studied in 1767-1771 in Leipzig at the same time as Goethe. In the second half of the 18th century, however, Russia was importing Germans, especially from Göttingen. Then from the beginning of the 19th century the Russian government in its endeavours to create Russian scholars and teachers systematically sent academic youth to the famous German universities for 'perfection in sciences and preparation for the professional occupation', as official language described it. Men of the Russian nobility often undertook trips to Germany on their own volition, for study at the universities, to get acquainted with German institutions, and to compare them with those of other parts of Western Europe. Trips to continental Europe usually led through Germany, which especially in 1813-1815 became a passing camp for Russian officers.

The scholarly standing of German universities, the romanticism of the student life in the small university cities, and their academic freedom in the early 19th century appealed not only to the Russians but to academic youth all over the world.

In the Russian case it was especially the nobility and the bureaucracy who sent their sons to the German universities early in the 19th century; but also the politically left and revolutionary youth in its permanent conflicts with the Russian administration usually received higher education in German universities and training in revolutionary thought in the emigrant colonies. For emigrants of the Russian left, only Switzerland could somehow compete with the attraction (but not with the influence) exercised by the German universities. Even Paris played in this respect a secondary role.

In the first quarter of the 19th century the University of Göttingen was the special magnet for Russian youth. Napoleon was correct in stating once that Göttingen belonged not just to Germany but to all Europe: at that period it was *the* university of Europe. One can hardly imagine today the cosmopolitan spirit

[68] A. Brückner, *Die Europäisierung Russlands,* Gotha, 1888, p. 247.

and scholarly standing of the University of Göttingen in the twenties of the previous century.[69]

Speaking in the sixties of the influence of economics on the life of modern Europe, Bezobrazov emphasized: 'At that period the University of Göttingen was the one among all the German seats of higher learning which could best prepare young talents for state careers; especially because independently of jurisprudence, instruction in political sciences was conducted there with a remarkable success due to professors like Achenwall, Schlözer, and Spittler'.[70]

Flocks of talented youth from far-off corners of the world hurried to this source of wisdom and knowledge. It was the deliberate policy of this university at that period to attract young foreigners, especially from England.[71] The Russians were conspicuous in their international milieu. Pushkin immortalized this period in the portrait of 'Vladimir Lensky with a soul from Göttingen', educated under the 'skies of Schiller and Goethe'—a portrait also covering the second period of Russian peregrinations to Germany, of exaltation of German philosophy and admiration for Schelling.

When N. I. Turgenev went in 1808 to Göttingen, he travelled in the company of twelve students of the Pedagogical Institute of St. Petersburg who were being sent to Germany. Among them were Galitch, who became an outstanding philosopher; the political scientist Kunitsyn (he later spent some time in Paris);[72] and future professors of political economy at St. Petersburg Plisov (who later went to Heidelberg) and Butyrski. Another Russian student in Göttingen who, like Turgenev, was not sent by the government but went at his own expense, was A I. Mikhailovski-Danilevski, later the collaborator of Turgenev in government service. There also were in Göttingen at that time three young scholars sent by the University of Moscow and fifteen, as Turgenev called them, *Kurlandtsy* from the Baltic provinces. Professor Meiners of

[69] M. Wischnitzer, *Die Universität Göttingen und die Entwicklung der liberalen Ideen in Russland im ersten Viertel der 19. Jahrhunderts*, Berlin, 1907.

[70] Bezobrazov, *Memoires de l'Academie Impériale des Sciences de Saint Petersburg*, p. 45.

[71] The first migration of young American historians to Europe occurred about the same time; their destination was also Göttingen.

[72] Kunitsyn was one of the most popular professors at the Alexandrovski Lyceum and the University of St. Petersburg. Pushkin dedicated to him the famous lines:

> To him the offerings of Heart and Wine;
> In our souls the flames of love he lighted,
> He laid the cornerstone, the ship he lighted
> He brightly made the lamp of wisdom shine.

Galitch had a similar influence in the lyceum.

Göttingen was the principal counsellor of M. N. Muravyev, then the curator of Moscow University, of which Turgenev's father was director.

Göttingen was the bridge over which Smithianism continued to cross to Russia. Of course, as we have seen in Chapter II, for a period of time there was a direct English influence in Russia, there were direct personal relations with England and direct transplantation of English ideas; but Göttingen was responsible for the enlargement and strengthening of the stream of Smithianism in Russia. The teachers of economics at Göttingen at that time were outspoken followers of the English master. Thus, Professor George Sartorius' first edition of *Von den Elementen des National-Reichtums und von der Staatswirtschaft* (Berlin, 1796) had a subtitle: 'developed according to the principles of Adam Smith'. Its second edition (Göttingen, 1806) was translated into Russian in 1812 by an adjunct professor of Kazan University, Peter Kondyrev. The conception of natural law was represented in Göttingen by the famous Hugo and a group of younger professors of the faculty of law, like Heeren and Göde. The only representative of the old cameralist school was Professor Beckman, instructor in 'science of commerce' (*Handlungswissenschaft*), who had previously been a teacher at St. Peter's School in St. Petersburg.

The Russian students followed in the steps of Sartorius. Mikhailovski-Danilevski's archive, preserved in the Public Library of St. Petersburg, contained seminar papers prepared for Sartorius along the lines of pure Smithianism. The archive of Prince Gorchakov (classmate of Pushkin in the lyceum and the future *célèbre* minister of foreign affairs) contains notes on Kunitsyn's lectures 'according to Adam Smith'. We discussed in Chapter II the Smithianism of Turgenev's *Theory of Taxation,* the Göttingen origin of which is now clarified. Turgenev even was accused by enemies of using Sartorius' class notes for this publication. The political ideas of Turgenev reflect Göttingen probably no less than did his training in economics. Here showed the influence of Freiherr von Stein, with whom Turgenev later collaborated in the war for liberation, and whose reforms impressed the young Russian liberal.

Even in later years Göttingen's influence was noticeable in the development of Russian economics. Several future professors of the University of St. Petersburg spent their student years at Göttingen, among them A. T. Kranichfeld, A. B. von Buschen (who contributed to the *Tübinger Zeitschrift für die Gesamte Staatswissenschaft*), F. N. Panov, V. A. Lebedev. Missions to Germany from Moscow resulted in an unusual crop of great scholars in the field of social sciences, among them Redkin, Leshkov, Krylov, Barshev, Chivilev.

Not less important was the next migration of Russian students to Germany in the second quarter of the 19th century. The attraction at this time was German romantic philosophy. Schelling was the idol of young Russian philosophers.

Even N. I. Turgenev, who did not develop special interest in philosophy but liked to keep up to date with current and fashionable trends (he attended J. B. Say's lectures at the Sorbonne, in this way getting acquainted with the French brand of Smithianism), took an opportunity to make the personal acquaintance of Schelling (in Karlsbad in 1825).

The second migration had a rather indirect influence on the evolution of economic thought in Russia. It inspired the 'German sentimentalists' who opposed the 'French *frondeurs*', and became one of the mainstays of Russian nationalist theories in economics, theories opposing the West and denying its culture, theories looking back to the patriarchality of Russian past. We shall investigate these in Chapter V.

Official missions of young Russian economists to Germany were replaced during Nicholas I's administration by studies in the Professorial Institute in Dorpat especially formed upon the proposal of Professor Parrot. In many cases, nevertheless, residence in Dorpat was followed by educational trips abroad.

Not less important than the migration of students to Germany was the importation of German professors to Russia, as well as migrations on their own initiative. A colourful gallery of German economists found its way to Russia at the beginning of the 19th century.

Christian von Schlözer, son of the historian August Ludwig von Schlözer of Göttingen, had the chair of political economy in Dorpat, 1800; in Moscow, 1801-1826; and after 1826, at Bonn,[73] where Grellmann and later Heym taught statistics (about 1806-07). Christian von Schlözer advocated Smithianism in his professional lectures as well as in his two volumes of *Anfangsgründe der Staatswissenschaft oder die Lehre von National-Reichtum* commissioned by the curator of the university Muravyev and published in 1805-07 in Riga.[74]

Heinrich Friedrich von Storch, born in Riga of German parents

[73] His father left Russian service, considering that its conditions conflicted with the role and duties of a historian. He tutored in the Rasumovski Educational Institute. Upon his return to Göttingen he supervised the work of Russian students.

[74] Karl Rau declared it to be the best contemporary textbook.

in 1766, studied in Jena and Heidelberg and was professor of political economy at the Academy of Sciences in St. Petersburg; he developed the theory of the 'transit', or go-between, character of early Russian commerce.

Storch lectured to the emperor Alexander I and to the future emperor Nicholas I; nevertheless, the censorship prevented a Russian translation of his main work, *Course d'économie politique*, published in French in St. Petersburg in 1815. Following Adam Smith and presenting numerous data on Russia and illustrations from Russian economic life, Storch was in some ways a forerunner of Ricardo in the theory of rent and the quantitative theory of money. He dedicated brilliant pages to discussing the advantages of free labour.

Karl Hermann, born in Danzig, studied in Göttingen and entered Russian service in 1795. He was appointed professor of statistics and geography. Hermann, as was illustrated in a previous chapter, was the favourite teacher of the Decembrists; he inspired Russian youth, and especially the young professors, with ideas of freedom. His student Professor Arsenyev, and his colleagues Galitch, Raupach, Kunitsyn, and several others, were persecuted after 1821 and up to 1827 by the administration. Hermann's statistical works, as well as those of some of his colleagues, were banned.

Most of the above-mentioned German economists developed a slight opposition to the government. But there was a group of German Smithians working directly with the administration. It was the Speranski collaborators mentioned in Chapter II, headed by Balugyanski and Jacob.

The Carpathian Slav Mikhail A. Balugyanski, professor at the Pedagogical Institute, later dean and rector of the University of St. Petersburg, collaborator of M. M. Speranski, received his education at the University of Vienna and belonged to the group of imported economists.

Ludwig Heinrich von Jacob, professor and later rector at Halle an der Saale spent ten years (1806-16) teaching political economy at the University of Kharkov before returning to Halle. Like several other such migrators, Jacob was compelled to leave Halle as Napoleon closed the university. Jacob was the most philosophically inclined of the German economists in Russia at that time: he tried to combine in his teachings Immanuel Kant and Smith. He published in Russia his *Grundätze der Policeygesetzgebung und der Policeyanstalten* (Kharkov, 1809), in which he opposed serfdom. His work became known and influential in Russia although for similar statements a few years earlier books of another German

55

professor, Johann Baptist Schad, were ordered burned, and Schad himself was deported from Russia.[75] Jacob was later awarded a prize of the Imperial Free Economic Society in a competition on the topic: 'What kind of labour is more profitable to the landlords —that of serfs or of free men?' [76]

Teaching the principles of Smithianism, the German professors during their Russian residence—sometimes of many years—were influenced at the same time by local conditions and thought. Continental Russia was for these studious and diligent observers a lesson in the relativity of English economic theories, and several of the German Smithians in Russia (for instance, von Schlözer) clearly admitted this opinion. Slowly Russia became the sample case and school for developing German anticlassicism; German opposition to the English school of economics found support and new arguments in the study of Russian economic life, and Russians willingly and naturally joined this opposition camp.

Thus the two continental countries of Europe began a cross-fertilization of ideas and conceptions in their opposition to the leading insular industrial nation of the world.

It was not only geographical proximity and personal contacts: it was a certain *parallelism of interests of continental economies on the way to capitalism*, striving to develop their resources and preserve their economic independence which made common their opposition to the ideas of the classical school, the theoretical foundation of British supremacy.

German-Russian economists vividly realized the specific conditions of under- and undeveloped nations, and often—especially von Schlözer—compared the evolution of Russia with that of the United States, seat of another continental opposition against the domination of absolute English theories.[77]

A more consistent and unconditional opposition expressed itself best in the works of numerous German non-academic economists who found their way into Russia in the second quarter of the 19th century. The most original of them, while peculiar and often contradictory, was of course, Y. F. Kankrin, later Russian minister of finance and Russian count, who studied at Giessen and Marburg, went to Russia in 1797, and published his *Fragmente über die*

[75] Professor Schad had been engaged by the university upon the recommendation of Fichte, Schiller, and Goethe.

[76] L. H. von Jacob, *Uber die Arbeit leibeigener und freier Bauern in Beziehung auf den Nutzen des Landeigentümer vorzüglich in Russland,* St. Petersburg, 1814.

[77] Cf. my *Spirit of American Economics.* Christian von Schlözer was probably the first economist to emphasize certain similarities between the development of Russia and of the United States.

*Kriegskunst* in St. Petersburg in 1809. The title and contents of this work are typical of Kankrin. Wilhelm Roscher aptly remarked that 'while so many successors of Adam Smith theorized on the tacit assumption that all men are just correctly calculating economists and all states are peace establishments, Kankrin seemed inclined to assume permanent wars, or at least permanent war preparedness'.[78] Problems of war economy continued to attract Kankrin and he published in St. Petersburg in 1820-23 three volumes in German on *War Economy in War and Peace and Its Influence on Army Actions.*

The Russian free-traders did not approve of him. V. P. Bezobrazov stated that 'it is difficult to find opinions more opposed and more hostile to the most elementary principles of economic science, and to the genius of modern civilization as well, than those of Count Kankrin'.[79]

Kankrin resented the internationalism of the British and emphasized that national wealth has to serve the fulfilment of the chief aim of a nation: its independent and secure existence. He was critical of classical economics, and while in some ways similar to the mercantilists, he anticipated Friedrich List in stressing national interest. But Kankrin's search for equilibrium resulted in an emphasis on stability, changelessness: theoretically he opposed railroads, banks, any innovations—even being compelled sometimes as minister of finance to bypass his own theoretical concepts. His system found expression in two German books (he never learned the Russian language sufficiently well): *Weltreichtum, Nationalreichtum und Staatswirtschaft,* (St. Petersburg, 1821) and *Okonomie der menschlichen Gesellschaft* (St. Petersburg, 1845).

Theodor von Bernhardi (the future German *General-Major)*[80] in his opposition to the English classics was influenced by the German romantic economist Adam Müller. While Kantrin gave special attention to problems of war economy, von Bernhardi became one of the greatest German war experts. Von Moltke called him the best German strategist;[81] he was also a historian and diplomat. Von Bernhardi belonged intellectually to the young romantic movement in Germany. His mother was the sister of

---

[78] Y. F. Kankrin, *Fragmente über die Kriegskunst,* St. Petersburg, 1809, p. 169.

[79] Bezobrazov, *De l'influence de la science économique,* p. 69.

[80] Cf. Fritz Demuth, *F. Th. v. Bernhardi: Ein Beitrag zur Geschichte der Nationalökonomie im XIX., Jahrhundert,* Jena, 1900.

[81] It is rather interesting to note that the greatest German expert on warfare, von Clausewitz, was also in Russian service.

Ludwig Tieck. Born in Berlin, he studied at Heidelberg but spent a large part of his life in Riga and St. Petersburg.

Bernhardi's *Versuch einer Kritik der Gründe, die für grosses und kleines Grundeigentum aufgeführt werden,* published in St. Petersburg in 1849, is markedly anti-Smithian but even more anti-Ricardian. It calls for an organic understanding of the economy *(die Volkswirtschaft als Ganzes);* and in his opposition to the classical thinkers Bernhardi described McCulloch as 'the most prejudiced and narrow teacher of political economy'.

In later years there were still isolated cases of German economists' migrating to Russia for study. A peculiar figure was Karl Schmaltz, doctor of philosophy of the University of Königsberg, who presented in 1840 at the University of St. Petersburg a thesis in German *Uber Grundsteuer und die Methoden ihrer Umlage,* and received the degree of master of technology. In 1864 Alexander Brückner, doctor of philosophy of the University of Heidelberg, presented in St. Petersburg a Russian thesis on *Copper Money in Russia in 1656-1663 and Paper Money in Sweden in 1716-1719,* and received the degree of master of history.

German influence on Russian economics seems to be manifold. Germans advised the Government; they taught the youth; they published their studies on and in Russia. Sometimes they were affected by the Russian milieu; in any case their Russian students certainly absorbed the German atmosphere.

As we see, the administration and the opposition, and English classicism and the reaction against it, all had in Russia the same German source and inspiration. And we shall have occasion to learn in the next chapter that even the Slavophiles, in their opposition to Adam Smith and other classical economists, in their search for the Russian soul and their denial of the West, also drew heavily on German philosophy and economic theory.

With their usual love for systematizing and pigeon-holing, German historians of economic thought speak of a German-Russian school of economists in the first half of the 19th century. This theory originated in Wilhelm Roscher's already quoted report and became a standard opinion until more recently Hans-Jürgen Seraphim tried to demolish it.[82] I still think that Wilhelm Roscher was correct in observing a something common to most of the German economists who lived and studied in Russia: it was the influence of the Russian environment, conditions, and experience.

With the same right one can speak of a German-Russian school

---

[82] Hans-Jürgen Seraphim, *Neuere Russische Wert- und Kapitalzinstheorien,* Berlin u. Leipzig, 1925.

in the second half of the 19th century, when many of the future notables were beginning their careers or marking time in the Baltic provinces waiting for a call to some great university in the fatherland. Russia was just a transit station for them.

In Roscher's words: 'To be sure, none of them undertook great historical studies; rather, most of them came to Russia with the easy assumption that the rules learned at home, most of which, indeed, were suitable for an advanced stage of culture, would be valid anywhere in the world. Their practical sense, however, soon convinced them that this was not the case, at least in Russia. Accordingly they endeavoured to broaden the rules to cover Russia. At the same time, through unprejudiced statistical observation of the many different and often primitive cultures surrounding Russia, they began to recognize the relativity in time and place of numerous principles hitherto considered absolute.' [83]

In the first half of the 19th century the influence was mutual. German economists contributed to the development and teaching of economics in Russia and were influenced themselves by the Russian milieu. Their activity in Russia was not limited to the transplantation and dissemination of classical economics. Their role was probably more important in the early struggle against the domination of English theories. The theoretical ideas of the French Utopians and the practical programme of the second generation of their disciples became dominant in Russia in the forties and fifties. But it was only natural that, when the developing young native capitalism in Russia needed a theoretical formulation and a programme for application, the source of inspiration was again in German economics. Friedrich List's national system influenced the great Russian scientist D. N. Mendeleyev and the Russian statesman Count S. J. Witte. Even a superficial perusal of Mendeleyev's *Comprehensive Tariff, Theory of Industry, Toward Knowledge of Russia,* or his studies of the iron industry in the Urals, will disclose his emphasis on national economic emancipation and industrial development. Mendeleyev in his practical activity did not want to limit himself to work in the frame of a single —even the biggest—private enterprise: he preferred to serve the total national economy. (Many of Mendeleyev's ideas and projects were later executed and glorified by the Soviet Union, especially his favourite theme of including North Arctic regions in the national economic system.) Count S. J. Witte openly acknowledged his dependence on Friedrich List in his *Synopsis of Lectures on*

[83] *Ibid.*, p. 140.

*National and State Economy.*[84] List's thorough revision of all the notions of the English school corresponded at that time to the demands and interests of Russian national capitalist development. No wonder that Count Witte happened to be the author of a study *About Nationalism: Friedrich List's National Economy.*[85]

The short-lived period of laissez faire in the sixties evaporated In the second half of the 19th century we encounter a Russia dominated by German influence in theory and practice. German economic and political power strengthened the old relationship. The official Russian reactionary policy obediently followed and imitated German bureaucracy; the academic teachers admired German achievements; the rise of the German labour class and the spread and strength of Marxian teachings exercised their influence on Russian intelligentsia, labour, and revolutionary youth. Both left and right wing of German economics were opposed to absolute English teachings. German industry and German labour were in complete agreement in this direction: the new historical and socialist schools were unanimous in their understanding of modern capitalism as a historical and not a logical category.

Academic teachings in Russia adopted at that period the main lines of the German historical school. Robert von Mohl and Karl H. Rau were elected honorary members of the University of St. Petersburg in 1861; Lorenz von Stein in 1869. The main representative of this trend in St. Petersburg was I. I. Yanzhul, author of *English Free Trade,*[86] and in Moscow A. I. Chuprov (disciple of Babst), the notable chairman of the Statistical Section of the Moscow Juridical Society and one of Babst's colleagues in publishing (in its early years) that mainstay of Russian academic liberalism, the daily *Russian Reports.*[87] Chuprov's *Lectures on Political Economy,* first mimeographed by his students and later revised by him and published, remained for almost three decades *the* textbook. And only at the beginning of the 20th century did it meet some competition on the part of a semi-Marxian textbook,

[84] S. J. Witte, *Synopsis of Lectures on National and State Economy,* St. Petersburg, 1912.

[85] S. J. Witte, *About Nationalism: Friedrich List's National Economy,* 2nd edition, St. Petersburg, 1912.

[86] I. I. Yanzhul, *English Free Trade,* 2 vol., Moscow, 1876-1882.

[87] No other country in the world ever possessed a daily periodical of similar standing and level. This long-established Moscow paper was closed in 1918. It was less informative than the *Frankfurter Zeitung* but more erudite. Chuprov's son, Professor A. A. Chuprov, the statistician, was one of its last editors. It is difficult for a foreigner to understand the importance of this periodical in clarification of Russian economic problems. I contributed regularly to its economic section in the years 1910-1918.

*Sketches on Political Economy* by V. Y. Zheleznov, who taught first at Kiev and later at Moscow.

Yanzhul and Chuprov adopted the German *Kathedersozialismus*, and the majority of Russian academic economists of this period followed them. Of course, this was not a straight transplantation of the ideas of the historical-ethical school. Chuprov's teachings were blended with some notions of Rodbertus; A. S. Posnikov (the first dean of the Department of Economics, and later director of the St. Petersburg Polytechnicum) played with some injection of Ricardo into the historical school; traces of popularized Marxism were to be found in many cases, as well as an addition of Austrian marginal theories. But historism of the Schmoller type dominated. Young scholars again went to Germany: Schmoller, Adolf Wagner, Brentano, Lexis, Karl Bücher, Knapp, and von Schulze-Gaevernitz were the German teachers most popular among young Russian economists. It was a matter of course for them to publish the results of their research in German economic periodicals. In Russia itself began an age of monographs on the model of German dissertations.

German hegemony manifested itself clearly in the organization of the first department of economics in Russia—at the Imperial St. Petersburg Polytechnical Institute (1903). A large part of the instructors were German trained, most of them belonged to the historical school and combined their historism with some Marxism and Populism. Of course, it was to Germany they sent their disciples. As far as the quality of teachers and students in this Polytechnicum, organized by Count S. J. Witte upon the suggestion of the great chemist Mendeleyev, was concerned, it was a brilliant school. Ten years after its establishment one could already notice the penetration and influence of economists from the Polytechnicum in all branches of administration and economic activity as well as in economic research. But despite all attempts to imitate the habits and traditions of an English college, it remained in substance a Russian university under German influence.

Only in agrarian problems did most of the Russian professors keep to the autochthonous standpoint of Populism, with the theory of which we shall become acquainted later. That was the case of A. S. Posnikov, of N. A. Kablukov, A. A. Manuilov, A. F. Fortunatov, V. A. Karyshev, A. I. Skvortsov, A. P. Lyudogovski, I. E. Yanson, M. J. Gertzenstein, and many others. A Russian school of public finance along German lines was developed and headed by I. Ch. Ozerov (of the universities of Moscow and St. Petersburg) and continued by his numerous students. Seminars of German type were successfully introduced by J. M. Goldstein at the University of Moscow.

The greatest success was achieved in Russia by the discipline of statistics. The influence of Quetelet was strong, especially in the middle of the 19th century. Later on theoretical studies by D. Zhuravski, I. I. Kaufmann, A. A. Kaufmann, and especially by the great A. A. Chuprov (his influence spread rapidly all over Europe) found a practical counterpart in numerous factual investigations. In the last quarter of the 19th century the statistical departments of the units of local self-government *(zemstvo)* had come to occupy a prominent place as schools for Russian statisticians and economists. We find here the names of W. I. Orlov, N. F. Annenski, Shcherbina, A. A. Rusov, and many others, most of them combining the historical ethical current with a brand of Populism.

German socialism replaced in Russia after 1848 the French brand so buoyant in the thirties and forties. Lasalle and Stirner had a certain following in Russia, but Marx and Engels practically conquered the country; and the philosophical foundation of Hegel and Feuerbach became the common faith of Russian progressive society. The radical intelligentsia and especially the youth became infatuated with German Marxism in all its colourings and factions. There are many fascinating pages in this development where one encounters loves and hatreds, fidelity and perfidy, grandeur of thought and petty jealousies, independence of mind, intellectual revolts and intellectual slavery, military discipline, and factional anarchy.

The formal history of Marxism's penetration into Russia is well known. Less attention has been given to the fascination it exercised over the Russian intelligentsia. One of the foremost Russian economists of the transition from the 19th to 20th centuries, S. N. Bulgakov, professor of Kiev and later at Moscow, who moved from Marxism to idealism and is now ending his earthly life as a monk in France, stressed that 'one who felt it, will never forget the initial fascination of Russian Marxism'; he described how after the depressing eighties Marxism became a 'source of courage and active optimism, the militant slogan of young Russia, its social ferment'; how in the nineties Marxism became popular among the intelligentsia.[88] Scientific Marxism gave satisfaction to the Russian striving for the absolute. Nicholas Berdyaev, who underwent a similar intellectual process and is now preaching a return to the Middle Ages, stressed that 'the rise of Russian Marxism was a

---

[88] S. N. Bulgakov, *From Marxism to Idealism*, St. Petersburg, 1903. p. vii.

serious crisis for the Russian intelligentsia, a severe shock to the foundations of their general outlook on life'.[89]

The pedigree of Russian Marxism leads us back to the end of the first half of the 19th century. In the forties Belinski, Herzen, Annenkov, Botkin, and several others became acquainted with Marx's early writings.[90] In the fifties and sixties Chernyshevski, Dobrolyubov, Shelgunov already studied Marx. In 1862 Bakunin translated the *Communist Manifesto*. P. N. Tkachev used Marx's formula in 1865; he was one of the first to talk about Marx; in 1875 he wrote a letter to Engels about Russia's own particular line of development and about the special character of the coming revolution.

We encounter the first academic mention of Marx in N. I. Ziber's *David Ricardo and Karl Marx* followed by his *Ricardo's Theory of Value and Capital*;[91] a Russian translation of the first volume of *Kapital* by Nicolai-on (Danielson) appeared in 1872 (the second and third were translated in 1885 and 1896); the *European Messenger* published in 1877 Zhukovski's debate with Marx. In 1883 Plekhanov formed in Geneva the first Russian Marxian organization named 'Liberation of Labour'.

The well-known memoirs of P. V. Annenkov previously mentioned, while not always reliable, present a vivid picture of Marx's first contacts with Russians.[92] The Russian political emigrés were constantly (and especially after 1848) meeting German emigrants all over Europe; they formed contacts with all 'Young' movements of the period and felt at home in revolutionary circles in Paris, London, and Switzerland.

Marx himself was rather surprised by his early success in Russia. In a letter to Annenkov (of March 28, 1846) dealing with Proudhon's *Système des contradictions économiques* Marx used the expression *sensiblerie sociale* and *socialisme moutonnier*. That was the way he probably felt toward the 'visions' of European socialism which aroused the curiosity of his Russian visitors. Marx preserved for a long time this attitude toward his Russian followers. He was

[89] N. Berdyayev, *The Origin of Russian Communism*, English translation, London, 1937, p. 113.

[90] Ryazanov described this stage of Russian acquaintance with Marx in his *Karl Marx and the Russians of the Forties*, Petrograd, 1918.

[91] Son of a Swiss immigrant, Ziber returned to Switzerland after two years of teaching at the University of Kiev.

[92] No one of the Russian writers of that period was personally acquainted with the Western socialist movement as well as was Annenkov. He attended on Marx's invitation the historic conversation of Marx and Engels with Weitling; he corresponded with Marx. Annenkov broke up the relationship after the revolutionary year 1848. Lavrov mockingly described Annenkov as a Russian "aesthetical tourist" in Western Europe.

hostile toward official Russia as well as toward Russian revolutionaries.[93] The story of his relations with Bakunin is well known.

Looking back in 1868 at this period, and probably recalling his several disappointments with Russian visitors, Marx still expressed distrust over Russian interest in his teachings. He wrote to Kugelman (October 1868): 'It is an irony of fate that the Russians, whom I opposed for twenty-five years not only in German but also in French and English, always favoured me.' Marx stressed the admiration for his teachings on the part of Russian aristocrats in Paris, sales of his writings in Russia, and the fact that Russia was the first country to translate his *Kapital*. His explanation was that the Russian aristocracy usually got its early education in German universities and in Paris and ever afterward pursued the extreme Western currents. Marx called this interest 'pure gastronomy of the type cultivated by certain groups of the French aristocracy in the 18th century.

In later years Marx and Engels studied Russian in order to read original Russian works and especially to examine Russian statistical investigations. Marx mentioned this fact in some of his letters to Nicolai-on, to Sorge, to Kugelman and others. Later Marx became involved in arguments with the Narodniki. In 1887 we find in *Contemporary Notes* Marx's letter to the editor. Marx was correct in the understanding that his influence in Russia remained at the beginning purely individual.

Changing economic conditions prepared a more solid foundation for Marx's influence in Russia at the time of V. G. Plekhanov's entrance in the field. N. Flerovski's investigation on *The Situation of the Labour Class in Russia* [94] as well as a later, entirely forgotten, study by V. Skaldin, *In the Sticks and in the Capital*,[95] exercised strong influence in the seventies and eighties, and prepared the soil for Russian Marxism.

Not only was Plekhanov the great Russian theoretician of Marxism, but he applied Marxism to the Russian actuality.

A Narodnik at the beginning of his activity, Plekhanov fought the Narodniki from his exile and stressed that the further develop-

[93] "The irresistible influence of Russia reached suddenly to Europe in various epochs and caused fear among the nations of the West which obeyed it like fatum or resisted in convulsions." Karl Marx, *Secret Diplomatic History of the 18th Century*, London, 1899. First published under the title *Revelations of the Diplomatic History of the 18th Century* in *The Free Press*, 1856 (VI) and 1857 (V).

[94] N. Flerovski (V. V. Bervy), *The Situation of the Labor Class in Russia*, St. Petersburg, 1870. Quoted by Marx in his correspondence with Engels, volume IV.

[95] V. Skaldin, *In the Sticks and in the Capital*, St. Petersburg, 1870.

ment of capitalism was in the interest of the working class as it prepared the ground for socialism. His pseudonyms 'Beltov' and 'Volgin' were popular among the Russian intelligentsia. His objections to the subjective sociology of Mikhailovski made a strong impression.

The Marxian Social Democratic Party of Russia soon embraced more than the labour class advance guard; it was successful in permeating larger layers of Russian society. The growing bourgeoisie, in common with Marx's followers, realized the necessity of emphasizing the development of productive forces and the overthrow of the remaining features of the feudal system supported by tsarism.

The new professional classes joined the striving for political liberty and for expansion of productive forces, involving the growth of the capitalist form. Berdyayev pointed out that 'the first Russian Marxists were very fond of talking about the development of material productive forces as the chief ground of their hope and confidence. Thus they were interested in the actual economic development of Russia, not as a positive aim and a boon in itself, but because it supplied them with weapons for the revolutionary conflict. Such was their revolutionary psychology. The aims of the Russian intelligentsia to all appearances remained the same, but they acquired a new weapon for the conflict; they felt the ground firmer under their feet. Marxism was a more complex intellectual theory than those upon which the revolutionary intelligentsia had hitherto relied, and required greater intellectual power.[96]

The labour class considered the rise of capitalism an unavoidable stage of development, and supported its early advent in order to accelerate the victory of socialism.

The social basis of Russian Marxism, as we see, was not uniform in the last quarter of the 19th century. It was composed of temporary allies among whom the agrarian masses were absent. The Russian agrarian problem led to formation of a special brand of socialism—Russian Populism. We shall discuss in the next chapter this phase of Russian economic thought, which equally found its inspiration in German sources. What is important at this stage is to note the development of a permanent separation and conflict between, on one hand, the Populists and the agrarian Social Revolutionary party which replaced the early Populists, and on the other hand, the Social Democratic party representing orthodox Marxism.

Before long the left wing of the bourgeoisie and intelligentsia

[96] Berdyayev, *op. cit.*, p. 112.

E

joined forces against orthodox Marxism. The literary leadership of this opposition was in the hands of young academic economists.

German revisionism, started by Eduard Bernstein, found a strong echo in Russia.[97] It resulted in the formation of what the orthodox Marxists in Russia labelled 'legal Marxism', 'economism', and 'Brentanism'.[98] This trend originated in the first half of the nineties and was initiated by Peter von Struve's militant *Critical Notes on the Development of Capitalism in Russia*,[99] which caused a great controversy passionately discussed in the historical meetings of the Imperial Free Economic Society. N. Berdyayev, M. I. Tugan-Baranovski, and S. N. Bulgakov shared Struve's position at this time. Leo Buch's *Elements of Political Economy* [100] was even supplied with an introduction by Eduard Bernstein.

Lenin, under the pseudonym K. Tyulin, attacked the new current in his 1895 study *Materials for a Characterization of Our Economic Development,* which was barred by the censors. Lenin defined Struve's legal Marxism as 'reflection of Marxism in the bourgeoisie literature', and Lenin's *Spark* called Struve's periodical *Liberation,* published in Stuttgart, and his 'economism' an opportunist movement adjusted to the interests of the liberal bourgeoisie.

Plekhanov accused the opposition of trying to revise the theory of Marxism in order to abolish its revolutionary dialectics. In its attempts to emancipate itself from Marxism, the Russian intelligentsia looked for a refuge in German idealism. Hegel and Kant were the poles of Russian intellectual fluctuations. Bulgakov, Berdyayev, Struve—all of them made the complete circle from Marxism to idealism, remaining captives of German theories all the while. Russian revisionism expressed the return from materialism to philosophical idealism.

The battle cry 'back to idealism' was joined by jurisprudence (P. Y. Novgorodtsev); in literature it found its expression in the 'Neo-Idealism' and 'Neo-Romanticism' of Merezhkovski, Akim

---

[97] "The old intelligentsia, the kin of Vissarion Belinsky and the 'circles' of St. Petersburg and Moscow, was revolutionary in every fibre. It was academic, philosophical, literary, but it produced the fiery spirits of the seventies and eighties. The economic developments of Sergius Witte created, out of it, or side by side with it, another, a new intelligentsia, of managers, engineers and technicians. These were the men to whom the Revisionist Marxism of Eduard Bernstein, with its quietistic and anti-revolutionary philosophy, made its principal appeal. They had no sympathy with the Bolsheviks, dreaded the proletarian insurrection against authority." John Maynard, *The Russian Peasant,* p. 155.

[98] They referred to Lujo Brentano's attack on Karl Marx.

[99] P. von Struve, *Critical Notes on the Development of Capitalism in Russia,* St. Petersburg, 1894.

[101] L. Buch, *Elements of Political Economy,* St. Petersburg, 1902.

Volynski, and other leaders of then fashionable currents. Sooner or later the entire group of Russian academic Marxists of the nineties went through this crisis. The symposium *Problems of Idealism* edited in 1902 by Novgorodtsev was their manifesto. Some of them developed mystical and theological theories; for instance, Berdyayev, Bulgakov, and—in smaller degree—Struve.

There were few of them who, like Tugan-Baranovski, continued to consider themselves Marxists. Tugan-Baranovski, whose real strength as an economist was in his investigations of English industrial crises and of the history of Russian industry, worked on a synthesis of Marxism with Austrian theories of value.

Opposing orthodox Marxian theory, the Russian revisionists and future idealists attempted to combine the social-political demands of Marxism with the empiricism of the German historical school. (S. N. Bulgakov admitted it, prior to his escape into religious philosophy.) In reality they developed into a Russian version of the German *Kathedersozialismus* with a blend of native mysticism.

This fight between materialism and idealism became the main feature of Russian intellectual evolution in the 20th century up to the First World War. The symposium *Landmarks* was the manifesto of the former Marxists and new idealists; Berdyayev, Bulgakov, Gershenson, Isgoev, Kistyakovski, Struve, Frank were the contributors.

It is not within the scope of this study to write a history of economic literature in Russia; but the important contribution of the academic revisionists to the development of economics in Russia should not be neglected. They put methodological clarifications on the programme; they carried on historical studies; they brought into economics a broad philosophical background; they were up to date, acquainted with Western trends of thought (Peter von Struve probably had no rival in Western civilization in erudition and historical and philosophical broadness of horizon).[101]

---

[101] Intellectual fluctuations and peregrinations often reaching the force of a crisis used to be a regular feature of the history of the restless Russian intelligentsia. I think that the intellectual life of Peter von Struve could be presented as a typical case: from orthodox German Marxism to revisionism and idealism (the *Landmarks)*, to "K.D." (party of Constitutional Democrats), to extreme nationalism. imperialism, preaching of Great Russia and a hatred of Germans, to religious and mystic meditations and extreme reactionism during the emigration from Russia. In exile during Tsarism, in exile during Bolshevism; member of the Duma during the brief constitutional episode, head of the Foreign Economic Department during World War I, minister in the "white" Wrangel government, close collaborator in Braun's *Archiv für Sozialwissenschaft and Sozialpolitik*, editor of the revolutionary *Liberation* in Stuttgart, collaborator in the symposium *From*

They influenced the young generation of economists in Russia; they stimulated investigations of Russian economic problems; they were the first Russian university professors of economics in the Western sense. It was a historical irony that many of this group were dismissed or not admitted to teaching by the tsarist government and were only for a limited time in their activity connected with universities.

Thus the Russian road into the school of capitalism as well as into the school of socialism led through Germany. The new bourgeoisie, the new professional class, young labour, the new revolutionary youth—all of them looked to the German neighbour for guidance and inspiration. The French revolution stimulated the Russian nobility; but the *raznochintzy* of the second half of the 19th century borrowed from Germany. The 19th century in the evolution of economic thought in Russia resulted in an almost complete hegemony of German ideas. Bureaucracy, academic teaching, intelligentsia, and labour were equally affected by them. Marxism and the German ethical historical school won the battle in Russia.

The orthodox Social Democrats and the revisionists in their quarrels on Russian soil were, even more than in Germany, dominated by 'anguished care for the master's true teaching' (Nötzel). Even in their interfactional fights Russian Marxists were true to the German example, only exaggerating the differences and bitterness.

The interfactional fights led to the crystallization of problems and tactics; they also led to elimination of fellow travellers, to the formation of a centralized uniform organization, to the establishment of a strict party discipline. The history of Marxism in Russia has as milestones a series of schisms: the separation from Populists and Social Revolutionaries; divorce from the revisionists; and finally the schism in the Russian Social Democratic Party itself and its division in 1903 into Mensheviks and Bolsheviks. This schism was the beginning of emancipation from German influence. Plekhanov was the theoretical leader of Russian orthodox Marxism; he remained the head of the Mensheviks and was the leader in peacetime. In the revolution of 1917 the seemingly strong party of Mensheviks crumbled into dust. Lenin became the genius of Russian Bolshevism, its leader in war and peace.

---

*Marxism to Idealism,* editor of *Russian Though,* participant in the Slavophile symposium *Great Russia,* contributor to the *Moscow Weekly,* professor at the St. Petersburg Polytechnicum, member of the Russian Academy of Sciences, a great teacher and great scholar—in all his searches he remained brilliant, erudite, sincere, passionate, militant, and unstable.

# V. The Native Currents

One cannot understand Russia by reason
And measure her by common yardstick;
She has a peculiar way,
One has just to believe in Russia.
                              TYUTCHEV.

T H E previous chapter presented a picture of a steadily expand-
ing growth of German influence on the development of economic
thought in Russia. Russia willingly adopted German economic
theories as an ally in its opposition to the English classical school.
German Marxism helped Russia to emancipate itself from French
Utopian socialism. But in the background of all the theories German philosophy was constantly admired by the Russian intelligentsia of all shades and colourings of opinions.

Meanwhile the growth of Russian national consciousness
required and determined the appearance of a series of native,
'genuine' Russian currents as a reaction against Western influences
and specifically against the German. This reaction was inevitable.
It led first to a general opposition to the West, to Europe, and
developed a feverish search for and emphasis on national, native
Russian features as contrasting with and opposed to the Western
European; it manifested itself in elaborate conceptions of a special
historical mission of Russia and resulted in a kind of 'manifest
destiny', a religious belief in Russia's messianic future.

But again and again, one can trace a strong influence of German
inspiration and German sources in 'genuine' Russian theories.
German influence crept in from all sides. Even in their reaction
against it, the Russians of the 19th century used German theories,
which they adjusted for this purpose. It was a belated influence of
German emphasis on *Volkstum* in the period of the Napoleonic
Wars, and at the same time adoration of the feudal system and
striving towards emancipation from everything French. Even
Russian anti-Germanism was of German ancestry.

What were the native, 'genuine', national currents of Russian
social thought? It was the idea of Holy Russia as contrasted with
*la belle France,* dear old England, and *Deutsche Gründlichkeit.*

One would search in vain for rounded out, systematic, logical
economic systems. The 'genuine' currents were mostly matters of

69

emotion, of belief, of imitation; of applying, *a priori*, political and social systems. But our harvest of theories will be rich if we explore the entire edifice of 'Russianism' and attempt a mosaic-like collection of its economic concepts.

Russian native theories could be divided into several groups; but in spite of all their distinctions and factional hairsplitting they had one thing in common: sectarian faith in the unique ways of Russian development.

This survey is of necessity not an exhaustive one and intends to present only by means of illustrations the evolution and rise of nativism in Russian economic thought in the 19th century. Reactionaries and radicals, bourgeois and socialists, aristocracy and the lower classes, intelligentsia and the army, peasantry and workers, clergy and scientists, bureaucracy and revolutionaries, poets and philosophers, Russians, Jews, Poles, Armenians, Georgians—all classes, all groups, all nations of the Russian Empire participated in the heated discussions and passionately took sides in this struggle of ideas which coloured a large part of the 19th century and the beginning of the 20th. In these skirmishes and fights all of them sooner or later arrived at the common faith of Russian people: their country's destiny to solve mankind's social problems. They believed that both the historic past and contemporary conditions put Russia in a privileged position to perform *the* social revolution and undertake world leadership. And even most of the Westerners, bitterly opposing nativism and fighting the Slavophiles, sooner or later fell under the spell of Russian messianism.

The only group to whom these beliefs and emotions remained strange were the Russian orthodox Social Democrats, the Mensheviks, brought up in the German Marxian kindergarten. Philosophically it can be explained by the contrast of Hegel and Schelling: the rationalism and relativism of faithful orthodox Hegelians against the absolutism and *Naturphilosophie* of the disciples of Schelling.

It is easy to produce illustrations demonstrating traces of economic nativism even in the early history of the Russian Empire. One can find its messianic political trends in the political and religious visions of Moscow as the Third Rome, expressed as early as the end of the 15th century and developed into a historico-philosophical theory formulated by the monk Philoteus of Pskov. The *Book of Degrees* (about 1550) showed definite messianic trends. Moscow was called the Third Rome in the edict establishing the patriarchate in Russia. The conservative economic side of nativism was best expressed in the famous statement of the boyar Bersen Beklemishev in a letter to Maxim the Greek: 'whatsoever country changes its customs, that country does not last long'.

Yuri Krizânic certainly could be—and often is—presented as an early Slavophile. Political Slavophilism irradiated his writings. This Croatian theologian and political writer, who followed in his *Politica* the views of contemporary mercantilism, made a special trip to far-off Russia to preach the union of all Slavs and a union of the churches. It is irrelevant for our purpose whether he was an agent of Rome or not (the question is still being discussed in historical literature[102]); the fact is that he was one of the first economists in Russia passionately favouring 'admirers of the old', whom he called *starinniki*. Of this type, cases are numerous. We meet nativist tendencies in Pososhkov's writings; they found their expression in party conflicts in the time of Peter the Great. But all these isolated cases were just attempts to stop innovations, to prevent reforms from destroying the structure of old Muscovite Russia. Only the 19th century showed a constant stream of attempts to create a systematic ideology for economic nativism. Only the 19th century witnessed the rising power and national consciousness of the Empire of the Tsars, and only in the 19th century did the fear of a rapid spread of Western capitalist forms produce a fertile soil for frank or veiled Slavophile theories. Only in the 19th century do we find vested interests sufficiently strong for support of economic nativism and opposition to the intruding Western forms.

An examination of the sources of the native currents in Russian economic thought leads us to Johann Gottfried Herder. His *Ideen zur Philosophie der Geschichte der Menschheit*, published in Rega in 1784, builds a theory on national peculiarities in character, customs, and social structure among the ancient Slavs. Herder stressed that the histories of the West and of the Slavs are different. This great German scholar who resided several years in Riga discovered the 'Slavic spirit'. He drew attention to the folk songs and folklore of the Slavs and, as an admirer of Rousseau, eulogized their idyllic agricultural life. Herder thought that by reason of it a great historical future was the destiny of the Slavs.

The historian August Ludwig von Schlözer who, as already stated also resided several years in Russia, emphasized in his studies the special 'system of Slavic History'.

Schlözer and Herder discovered the Slavic world to the European civilization and to the Slavs themselves. Herder's theory found a

102 Cf. V. Valdenberg, *Political Ideas of Krizânic*, St. Petersburg, 1912.

strong echo especially among the Western and Eastern Slavs. The famous *Slávy dcera* (1824), Jan Kollár's great hymn glorifying Slavism and depicting the Germans as the hereditary enemy of the Slavs, was a logical application of Herder's theory, as were Fallmerayer's *Geschichte der Halbinsel Morea* (1830), which predicted the transfer of world domination from Latin and German nations to the Slavs, and von Baader's interest in the Greek Orthodox church.

The Russian intelligentsia adopted these ideas under the influence of Schelling's and Hegel's philosophies. Hegel taught that in each period a dominating nation is the bearer of the world spirit, and that the migration of the world spirit is practically the contents of world history. Obviously this trend of thought could easily be applied to the great Slavic nation.

The immediate influence on the development of economic nativism in Russia was Schelling's *Naturphilosophie*. It was a stream parallel to the general revival of European romanticism which penetrated literature and art, theology and philosophy, economics and politics. But in Russia especially it was a feature of the Russian intelligentsia's infatuation with German romanticism, which in its mainstream was constantly fed by the German philosophy of the *Sturm und Drang* period. The broad and complex romantic intellectual ferment at the transition from the 18th to the 19th century, its magnificent and manifold picture of opinions, tastes, and goals, penetrated all nations of Europe (of Europe only?) and extended its influence not only to literature but also to social disciplines and ways of life. It adopted peculiar colourings in each country, and Russia was conquered by its German brand. And again, as in the case of early migrations to Göttingen, we meet the Russians paying respects personally to their new idol, Schelling. Chaadayev began the series of peregrinations in 1825. P. V. Kireyevski followed in 1829 and his brother I. V. Kireyevski in 1830; we meet V. P. Titov discussing problems with Schelling in 1836, N. A. Melgunov in 1839, Prince V. F. Odoyevski in 1842 —to mention only the most important Russian visitors. Among themselves they discussed not without irony the 'Geheimrat von Schelling', but with the piety of disciples brought home his bust. We have Melgunov's testimony to the fact that Schelling on his part was full of sympathy for Russia and the Russians, and especially for Moscow, where his teachings were so in vogue. Schelling himself spoke of the Russian mission in world history.

A Schellingian circle of *lyubomudry* philosophers originated in Moscow even earlier—in 1823—and developed into a secret society. Its active participants were the brothers Kireyevski, Prince V. F. Odoyevski, Titov, Shevirev, Melgunov, A. I. Koshelev, Dm. Venevitinov, Roshalin. After December 14, 1825, the society ended its existence when Odoyevski, at the last meeting, with special solemnity burned the statutes and minutes of the group.[103]

I mentioned in Chapter III the two Moscow university circles of the early thirties baptized as 'French' and 'German'. The 'German', or philosophical, circle included many names afterwards of note, among them K. S. Aksakov, the Slavophile, Vissarion Belinski, the great publicist and literary critic, and Michael Bakunin, the anarchist, at this time known as a quixotic young army officer with a flair for philosophy. 'Literature, particularly poetry and the drama, as well as philosophy and philosophy in its application to literary criticism, occupied this group of ardent seekers. Sometimes they met in the house of Peter Chaadayev, Nicholas I's "madman".'[104]

Moscow Schellingism was an atmosphere full of historico-philosophical speculations concerning the world destiny of peoples, their providential missions, conceptions of nationalities and so on. Many of the admirers of Schelling decided that Russia must 'become more oriental'. We may say that the famous triad of the Slavophiles—Othodoxy, Absolutism, and Populism—found its philosophical inspiration in these German theories.

Of course, while adopting the religious moment of German romanticism the disciples based their theories around Greek Orthodoxy.

'At the heart of Slavophilism is Russian Orthodoxy and the Orthodox mysticism which is the essence of all Christian culture in the East. The first Slavophiles were men of the ancestral life, typical Russian landlords, racy of the soil, who had sucked along with their mother's milk their living convictions. They were bred in the ideas of the old Orthodox way of living, of the Christian peasant commune, and of the Christian patriarchal State, in which all things are framed, in ideal at least, to the pattern of father with children. In their Orthodoxy there was something of the spirit of the Schism and of the Old Believers, the same convictions of Russian Messianism which began with the idea of Moscow as the

---

103 The chair of philosophy was abolished at Moscow in 1826. But Professor M. G. Pavlov, whose fields were physics and agriculture, really was lecturing in introductory philosophy. He used to stand in the doors of the physio-mathematical division and stop the students, asking them questions: "You want to acquire knowledge of nature? But what is nature? What is knowledge?"

104 John Maynard, *Russia in Flux*, p. 174.

Third Rome, and was so deeply outraged when Tsar Alexis and the Patriarch Nikon adopted the Greek tradition in the liturgy, and again when Peter the Great established an upstart capital in a non-Russian land. It was expressed in Konstantin Aksakov's apostrophe to Peter: "Thou hast despised Russia and all her past. Therefore a seal of malediction is imprinted on all thy senseless work. Pitilessly thou has repudiated Moscow and has gone out to build apart from thy people, a solitary city. For thou and they could no longer live together".

'In the reverence of the Slavophiles for the patriarchal head of the Russian community there was mingled a dislike for intruding Byzantine and German elements, and in particular for the bureaucracy and the machinery of the State which Peter had imported. They had their ears attuned to the Liberty Bell of Novgorod the Great, and their eyes fixed on the parliament of Kiev, or on the independent Communes, and the free assembly of the Zaporozhian Cossacks writing their outrageous letters of challenge to the Sultan of Turkey. They idealized the life of the people, of the plain folk. They held that they should return to the people and be made whole by them on the soil of a common faith. They were the first of the worshippers of the people, of the Narod, as the Russians call, not the nation but the plain folk: and, anti-revolutionary themselves and upholders of a patriarchal autocracy, they were the first to institute that "going to the people" which played so large a part in subsequent revolutionary movements. In Moscow, always alien in spirit from Peter's capital, the reaction towards antiquity took extravagant forms. Leading Slavophiles put their trousers inside their high boots, and wore the shirt with the collar fastened at the side, or masqueraded in robes which caused the gaping peasants to take them for Persian merchants. Pan-Slavonic patriotism ran riot and it became a pose to adopt popular superstitions and sacrifice reason to antiquarian sentiments.'[105]

Many German economic ideas of romanticism, and certainly its spirit, found an echo in Russia. Even non-Slavophile Russian economists, even realists like Chernyshevski, accepted the fundamental idea of German romantic economics—the idea of totality of the economy, the idea of its organic character, the denial of the inorganic atomism so deeply rooted in the principles of the English classical school. Like Adam Müller, the Slavophiles insisted that man was unthinkable except in a totality of human affairs, except in relation to a living whole. The living whole was the nation, in which was embodied the spiritual solidarity of mankind.

[105] *Ibid.*, pp. 161f.

Germany fostered the national economic currents in Russia more directly by its 'discovery' of Russian native social institutions.

The man who discovered the native Russian economic features to Europe and presented them in a new light to the Russians themselves was Freiherr A. von. Haxthausen, who visited Russia in the forties and published his famous book in 1847.[106]

The old institutions of village community (*mir*) and of *artel* appealed to Haxthausen's social conservatism; he was the first to consider these features of Russian economic structure in connection with the social strivings of the West. From his standpoint, development of large-scale industry was a luxury unnecessary to Russia since it possessed the above-mentioned institutions. He idealized the patriarchal structure of Russian economy in the following way: 'No national or family group exists in Russia without a centre, without unity, head, father, master; for he is utterly indispensable to its life and existence. The Russian, if God has taken his father, creates one for himself! Even the free community elects its elder *(starosta)* and obeys him absolutely; he is not a delegate but their father, having full and natural authority.'[107]

While Herzen claimed that Haxthausen borrowed from K. Aksakov the conceptions of mir and artel, all Slavophiles gladly accepted this unexpected support from an illustrious foreign observer. Haxthausen himself reported in Volume II of his work *(Jung Russland)* his complete accord with the Slavophiles, most of whom he met personally in Moscow.

A similar standpoint was taken later by another foreign student of Russia, L. von Tengoborski, who argued that development of handicraft helped Russia escape from the *'sore* of the proletariat.'[108] Haxthausen strongly assisted the 'search for Russian ways' as his theories found ready followers among the generation of Slavophiles who used them as their economic background. One can apply to Haxthausen the words of a poem dedicated by Tyutchev to another German student of Russia, A. E. Hilferding:

> He was not a Slav by birth,
> But all Slavs adopted him.

However, Herzen's indignation expressed in the statement 'We finally got a German to introduce us to Europe. Is it not a shame?'

---

106 A. von Haxthausen, *Studien über die innere Zustände, das Volksleben und insbesondere die ländlichen Einrichtungen Russlands,* Hanover, 1847.
107 *Op. cit.,* Bd. III, p. 150.
108 L. von Tengoborski, *Etudes sur les forces productives de la Russie,* Paris, 1852.

was, of course, exaggerated.[109] In reality the Russians knew their social institutions before Haxthausen, who only put the Western stamp of approval on the idea of their eventual role in the development of Russia's national economy, and emphasized their political importance.

Russian nativism existed, of course, prior to the Slavophiles and their use of Haxthausen's eulogy of the Russian mir and artel. Many of the Decembrists, in spite of the definitely Western character of the movement, played with native conceptions and forms. Ryleyev, Kakhovski, Küchelbecker, Prince A. I. Odoyevski (the cousin of V. F.), and even Pestel recollected the *Vieche* of Novgorod and the Russian *Zemskie Sobory*. Ryleyev arranged special Russian luncheons, and Küchelbecker longed to wear Russian national clothes at least in the countryside. They often used ancient Russian terminology, and thought of Moscow or Nizhni Novgorod as the future capital of Russia. The Society of United Slavs (1823) in alliance with the Southern Society was the centre of the Decembrist movement. We know that a 'Masonic Lodge of United Slavs' was formed in Kiev in 1818 and that the Kirill-Methodian Society (1846-47) was important in the development of Slavophilism. All of them were under the influence of German romanticism.

But even the economic teachings of the Slavophiles were not strange to some of the Decembrists. The same V. K. Küchelbecker in his 'European Travel Letters of an Inhabitant of North American States in the XXV Century' (published in 1820 in *Nevski Spectator* and *Fosterer of Enlightenment)* reported on the social structure of a Russian communal settlement inexplicably discovered in Italy. Typically for his attitude toward this patriarchal institution the name of the head of the settlement was Dobrov (Good man). The future leader of the Slavophiles, Khomyakov, became a frequent guest of Ryleyev's circle in the last few months of its existence, forming in this way a direct bridge between the Decembrists and the Slavophiles.

The Slavophile movement can be considered as an expression of Moscow atmosphere and trends. Of course, no strict topography of an intellectual movement is possible. Chaadayev, Granovski, Herzen—all of them Westerners—belonged to the society of Moscow; on the other hand, the magazine *Lighthouse*, which furiously

---

[109] V. P. Bezobrazov expressed the same complaint in a more general way, stating that the most important works on Russian economy and finances, like those by Storch, Haxthausen, Tengoborski, are a part of West-European rather than of Russian scholarship. *Op. cit.*, p. 69.

defended the ancient Russian institutions, was published in St. Petersburg. But generally speaking, the Slavophiles were typical of Moscow and the Westerners of St. Petersburg. The journal *Muscovite* was the centre of Slavophilism, and the *Contemporary Notes* of the Westernism of St. Petersburg. Moscow society accused St. Petersburg of being un-Russian. And Herzen's one-sided remark that St. Petersburg's distinction from all other European cities consisted in its similarity to all of them is in line with Moscow's accusation.

As P. V. Annenkov emphasized it in his *Literary Reminiscences* 'Moscow made a conservative opposition, based on the ancient principles of Russian culture, to St. Petersburg, which declared the bankruptcy of almost all Russian principles in comparison with the all-human, *i.e.*, European, development'.[110]

The Slavophiles were looking to the end of the 'St. Petersburg period' of Russian history (sometimes—admitting, as did I. V. Kireyevski, their own dependence on German philosophy—they called it the 'German period'); they were expecting the restitution of the 'genuine Russia'. They considered the Russian *narodnost* to be in the old Moscow. In this way historical theory amalgamated with local patriotism. Russian nobility remained during long periods continuously in their rural 'nests'—but intellectual life was awakening in these nests. These and Moscow gave birth to the Slavophile movement.

The philosophical theory of the Slavophiles was developed by I. V. Kireyevski, the historical by Konstantin Aksakov, the political by his brother Ivan, and the theological by A. S. Khomyakov.

All of them shared Kireyevski's faith in his spiritual and historical mission of Russia; all of them shared Kireyevski's repudiation of the revolutionary legacy and beliefs of the Decembrists; Kireyevski relied on German idealist philosophy, especially Schelling's, to support his political conservatism and approval of the Russian political structure. I. S. Aksakov taught that only denationalization of the Russian people would make it receptive to Western ideas. He was afraid that the 'spirit of the people' (typical German expression of the period) would not withstand the stress of coming capitalism.

All of them agreed that the Russian mir was a remarkable advantage of Russia in comparison with the West. A. S. Khomyakov in 1842, before Haxthausen discovered the Russian village community to the West, developed the idea that the communal land regime was peculiar to the Slavs and particularly to the Russians.

The economic part of the Slavophiles' theory was usually not considered by themselves to be an essential element of their teachings. The Slavophilism of the forties originated rather as an ethical-religious current somewhat coloured by a theory of a native Russian socialism as expressed in still-existing ancient Russian institutions. The Slavophiles were opposed to the West, to Western economic teachings, to Western socialism. Their Russian socialism consisted of the belief that mir and artel are the old Russian and future universal forms of collective possession and use of the tools of production. At the same time the Slavophile economic teachings were an echo of European waves of reaction against the liberalism of the classical school, and took the form of an idealization of the 'national' economy. The Westerner Chaadayev was one of the first to stress the 'retrospective Utopia' of the Slavophiles.

Meanwhile some of the speculations of the Slavophiles were slowly obtaining a realistic economic background. Emancipation of serfs, new means of communications, formation of a larger domestic market, and new credit organization prepared the conditions for the building up of a national industry. A new, growing national industry entered economic life, headed by the great Russian textile factories—more correctly, the cotton manufacturing industry of the Moscow region. This 'Lancashire of Russia' was its first large-scale modern industry in capitalist form. But while the interests of English Lancashire—the pioneer—requested an atmosphere of free trade and were represented by the English liberal bourgeoisie, the cotton industry of Moscow—a late newcomer—demanded protection; and the Slavophile tendency toward a *geschlossener Handelsstaat* (later revived by the great Mendeleyev) was more in tune with their new-born economic nationalism. In this way Moscow manufacturers made use of the idealist, quasi-socialist economic nativism propagated by the philosophizing intelligentsia; Slavophile ideas served Moscow industry as a defence against European competition, whose production technique it readily accepted. Moscow manufacturers used the Slavophile nativism as munition for their protectionist ideology. Slavophile ideas found allies in the young industry, while the parallel trend in Prussia became associated with the *Junkers*.

The next obvious step under this influence was a *transformation of the early Slavophilism into realistic political nationalism*. The end of the liberal period of Alexander II made Russian nationalism the mainstay of the new governmental policy. In the Russian-Turkish war of 1878 this 'Russian conception' found its official expression. Vladimir Solovyov dubbed its extreme manifestations 'zoological nationalism'.

The new nationalism was backed up by and theoretically based on the ideas of a decline of liberal Europe. Not only the conservative (or rather, traditionally anti-liberal) Germans, but also Englishmen like Disraeli and Carlyle, for instance, shared this belief at that time. The Pan-Slavists taught that Slavic culture overcame the individualism sickening Europe, and emphasized the Russian collectivist principle of *sobornost*.

Economic Pan-Slavism found its best expression in the writings of Yuri F. Samarin. Many of the Pan-Slavic theories had been expressed previously by Count Sergei S. Uvarov, one of the Göttingen students, later minister of education. The historian Michael P. Pogodin, one of the early collaborators of Odoyevski, Venevitinov, and Kireyevski, stressed the political factor more than the Slavophiles. But none expressed the economic reasoning of Pan-Slavism as clearly as Samarin, in spite of his being influenced by Khomyakov's theology.

Samarin presents one of the few cases of a direct discussion not only of economic problems but also of theories. In his refusal to be guided by English liberal economics Samarin was influenced by Friedrich List's system of national economy, which he combined with the traditional idealization of the Russian mir.

In a remarkable letter to Khomyakov in the fall of 1849 Samarin wrote that an extensive study of political economy had strengthened his belief that this discipline ('or more correctly—the series of conclusions based on the historical development of national economy in the West') deserved neither the disregard, newly developed by certain groups, nor the immense importance ascribed to it by those who thought of society as a joint stock company, national life as a business enterprise, and human existence as a digestive process. In its legitimate limits political economy can possibly be even useful. As for its practical application in Russia, in its present form it should be studied for self-education and not for the purpose of applying its prescriptions and recommendations presented as absolute truth.[111]

Thus Moscow manufacturing interests, through the 'retrospective Utopia' of the Slavophiles, found their tendency toward Friedrich List's economic nationalism favoured by the political chauvinism of the government and supported by certain groups of the intelligentsia.

It became customary in Russia to make a formal distinction

[111] Cf. B. E. Nolde, *Yuri Samarin and his Time*, Paris 1926, pp. 54f.

between Slavophiles and so-called Westerners. The actual development does not manifest this symmetry of contrasts. Generally speaking, one could search in vain for stability in the *Weltanschauung* of the Russian intelligentsia. The typical evolution is rather a constant search, constant change of 'landmarks' (to use a word in vogue in Russia at the beginning of the 20th century). One of the early Russian 'Marxists', N. Sazonov, even considered the 'lack of stability' and the 'mobility' of the Russian character to be special merits.

It is true that already in the forties the Russian intelligentsia (Annenkov, Botkin, Belinski) began to consider necessary the formation of a national bourgeoisie on the Western style. But most of them could not hide their fear of the advent of Western capitalist forms. A statement like V. P. Botkin's 'Lord, help us to have a bourgeoisie' was unusual and not typical in Russia. And even if Belinski repeated it, he soon abandoned it. The economic Westernism of the Russian intelligentsia has never been stable.

But there was one central idea common to Slavophiles, Pan-Slavists, and Westerners; the belief in the great future of their fatherland, in the historical mission of Russia, and its ethical, social, and political role in coming world reconstruction.

In many cases the Westerners joined the nativists in their refusal of the West: some occasionally, and others in a deliberate reversal of their former beliefs.

Let us consider the case of one of the first and leading Westerners—P. Y. Chaadayev. A mystic and philosopher in constant search of inner freedom and ethical liberty in opposition to positivism, a conservative resenting any extreme political revolution, he opposed the 'fanatical Slavs', as he called them. Chaadayev by his *Philosophical Letters* aroused the fury of Russian nationalists and brought upon himself persecution by the government, which declared him insane. He was full of pessimism in regard to Russia's past and present.

Chaadayev was of the opinion that Russia was not similar to the West European countries; that an extraordinary mission was her destiny, the peculiarity of her past development being a proof of it. Russia entirely separates itself from Europe. Europe has already disclosed its material potential. Russia must and can simply take over the ripe fruit of European efforts; this will give Russia the later possibility of coming near the final goal with such a rapidity that 'we will overtake the historically progressive Europe'; the guaranty of the future is not in the Slavophile past but in the present position. Chaadayev, the father of Russian historical scepticism, considered Russia too powerful and too big to be guided merely by national egoism. That her destiny was to lead an 'all-human' policy was the emphasis in his letters written between 1835 and 1837. And he never tired of repeating that while the central point of the problem is the relation between Russia and Western Europe, Russia should continue to live in its own manner, not imitating Europe but incessantly using the results of the long European experience in the way Peter the Great did. A Westerner, Prince V. F. Odoyevski, even prior to the appearance of Slavophiles as an organized group, was preaching that young Russia would bring salvation to ageing Europe. This thought can be traced to the idealist circles of the twenties; it blossomed in the time of Nicholas I. Distinguishing him from the Slavophiles, the 'European' is alive in Odoyevski, who does not manifest any intolerance toward the West; but the same Odoyevski developed a furious intolerance toward English political economy. He resented the theories of Bentham and Malthus, and often repeated in his *Russian Nights* that 'in the political economy the monstrous meaningless theories of Malthus' disgusted him; he fought Anglomania; he claimed that the famous English 'respectability' meant nothing but the possession of £20,000; he denounced the 'bankers' feudalism'; his Faust in *Russian Nights* simultaneously accused Western economic theories and Western forms of life, as Odoyevski insisted on their interrelation. Odoyevski hoped to lay the foundation of a 'new Russian political economy' or 'Russian social physiology' which would comply 'with strict scientific requirements as well as with the high principles of Christian ethics'.

Let us turn attention to a different trend of thought. N. A. Polevoi was a Westerner, a believer in the necessity of industrial development, one of the few active figures among the philosophizing intelligentsia of Moscow. V. F. Odoyevski's circle considered the publication of a periodical, and Polevoi with their approval started his famous *Telegraph*. The first polemics and arguments in the *Telegraph* brought snobbish remarks from the circle. They objected to the unacademic and even un-parlour-like style. ' It smells of lard and tar; prices of sturgeon are discussed; people quarrel and strike their unclean beards, tuck up their sleeves.' This description of the 'mercantile style' of the journal was just. A modern Soviet author, I. G. Blyumin, analysing Polevoi's idea, classifies him as one of the few representatives of the bourgeois interests of the period. It is true that Polevoi *the journalist* foresaw the coming industrialization of Russia and welcomed it; realized that Western capitalist forms were penetrating Russia. But deliberating on the

F

historical future of Russia, Polevoi *the historian* argues in his *History of the Russian People* that the role of Russia in the past was entirely different from that of the European West, and that it will have to remain distinct in the future.

Up to the last pages of his *History* Polevoi continued to stress that 'the future of Russia must be great', that Russia's destiny is to 'inject a peculiar spirit', that it is going to establish 'the type of an Eastern European formation' willed to Russia by dying Byzantium.

Alexander Herzen, who went through all the evolutionary phases of the Russian intelligentsia of his period, and led in many of them, could never free himself from the spell of Russian economic nativism despite spending, out of forty years of mature life, seven in banishment and almost twenty-five in exile. In early Moscow years Schelling's *Naturphilosophie* was his bible; in 1831-33 it was Saint-Simon; up to 1848 Herzen looked for the advent of socialism from the West; after 1848 he joined the 'peasant socialism' and considered the mir a safety valve against invading capitalism. As late as 1869 he still confronted Marx's teaching with his own 'peasant socialism'. His renowned open letter to Michelet contained, already, seeds of Slavophile theories. He went through periods of Utopian belief in the West ('We believe in Europe as Christians believe in Paradise') and of acute disappointment over the Western *Zukunftsstaat* as not applicable to Russia. Herzen arrived finally at a synthesis of Westernism and Slavophilism placing the mir in the centre of his plans of agrarian socialism, and stressing the economic aspects of this institution while orthodox Slavophiles emphasized the ethical. In contrast to liberal Westerners he found promise in the ancient Russian village community (the mir); in contrast to Slavophile traditionalists he looked for the mir to evolve into a socialist commune.

The foremost Westerner, Herzen, declared: 'Europe does not know us; it knows our government, our facade and nothing else'. In his *Bell* published in London, he hoped that the Russian 'barbarians' would bring their 'new faith' to a decaying Europe as the ancient barbarians brought Christianity to dying Rome. Any kind of Western liberalism—political or economic—became *bête noire* to Herzen. In a series of articles in the *Bell* (1859) typically entitled 'Russian Germans and German Russians' he fought the Russian Westerners who were willing to accept emancipation of peasants without land grants and did not object to the formation of proletarian masses and the growth of a bourgeoisie. Herzen dreaded the repitition of the Western petty bourgeoisie *(meshchanstvo)* on

Russian soil. He opposed capitalist development on Western European lines and stressed the primacy of a social and not a political revolution in order to avoid Western ways. Herzen looked forward to a combination of Russian customs and *mores* and Western science, and thought that in this way Russia was destined to avoid the capitalist form of development. Herzen called his theory 'Russian socialism' or sometimes 'Russian communism', and combinated in it the socialism of the muzhik and artel—agrarian socialism—with that of the urban worker. Herzen's synthesis became the foundation of Russian Populism of the seventies as well as of the future Social Revolutionary Party.

Not very much different was the case of Herzen's friend during his student period, the great critic and publicist, the Saint-Beuve of Russia, V. G. Belinski. Belinski is traditionally considered a pure Westerner. He went through the usual influence of Schelling, became interested in Fiche and Feuerbach; replaced Schelling by Hegel in 1836-37, gave up illusions of a peculiar beauty and ethics in archaic Russian institutions, and became one of the first advocates of Karl Marx in Russia. All these changes typify Belinski's perpetual infatuations and sincere enthusiasm. Thus in 1834 he declared that no Russian literature exists; in 1844 he admitted that Russian literature does exist. Belinski's slogan was 'sociality', emphasizing the primacy of social principles. Belinski believed in and foresaw a providential historical mission for Russia.

The same was the case of N. G. Chernyshevski, probably the ablest Russian economist of his time. In spite of the fact that he spent the years 1862-1888 in fortress, prison, forced labour, and banishment, his erudition was immense, his independence of thought remarkable. His *Notes on John Stuart Mill,* added to the Russian translation, testify to the brilliance and ripeness of his thought.

Chernyshevski in his teachings combined Feuerbach with Bentham and Mill; he tried to merge the English classical school and socialism; he introduced the 'anthropological principle' in philosophy and history. He was full of hatred and contempt for the bourgeoisie and for Western liberalism. His *Capital and Labour* is in this regard not less instructive than the introduction to the *Anthropological Principles* or his *Struggles of Parties in France*.

To some extent Chernyshevski anticipated Marx (whom he probably had not read before his imprisonment), especially in emphasizing the full development of productive forces as the way to socialism. He expected great immediate advantages for Russia from the victory of the engineer and manufacturer. But his socialism, like that of most Russians of that time, was of a distinctly ethical character. His famous Utopian novel *What To Do*, written in the fortress, called for the establishment of productive associations in Russia in the same year when Ferdinand Lasalle was recommending associations to German workers. But Chernyshevski was nearer to Schulze-Delitzsch than to Lasalle.

Chernyshevski was more of a scholarly realist than Herzen, with whom he disagreed on many points. Chernyshevski admitted the saviour role of the Russian mir. While realizing that it was not a specifically Russian or Slavic but rather an old European institution, he believed that this institution, still strong in Russia, would make the transition to communism especially easy; but he denied the dreams of an 'approaching decline of the decaying West'. It was his conviction that 'without convulsions there is no forward step possible in history'.

In this way, differently from Herzen, Chernyshevski the Westerner also arrived practically at a synthesis of the opposing theories, and joined the camp of believers in special ways of Russian economic development. The Russian messianic trend, too, was not strange to Chernyshevski. He visualized the future history in which 'Russians will appear not as conquerors and robbers like Huns and Mongols but as saviours'. The leitmotiv of unique social and economic development and of the Russian mission, which sooner or later combined, as we saw, the 'fanatical Slavs' and the Westerners, the 'Germans and sentimentalists' and the 'Frenchmen and *frondeurs*', the political reactionaries and the self-sacrificing revolutionaries, remained always alive, even with the Russian nihilists. I could not form a definite opinion in this direction concerning N. A. Dobrolyubov and D. I. Pisarev. The first, a collaborator and follower of Chernyshevski, did not live to see his twenty-seventh birthday and Pisarev, the most buoyant and brilliant of Russian nihilists, died at the age of twenty-eight.

Let us turn to one of the most picturesque and romantic figures of the 19th century, Michael Bakunin, the representative of 'careless nihilism', as Alexander Blok dubbed it. Bakunin was certainly the most colourful figure of the nihilist-anarchist episode in the development of Russian positivist and radical thought. His biography reads like a companion volume to I. S. Turgenev's social novels. Bakunin was full of conflicts and contradictions, of passion and erudition, of a drive for immediate activity and for knocking down all existing authorities, of devoted friendships and embittered animosities, very often reversing themselves. The victory of Russianism over internationalism has never and nowhere been so dramatically clear as in the case of Michael Bakunin. This born revolutionary who fought all over Europe for a new social order, for economic and political justice as he understood them, was constantly held in suspicion by Marx and others as a thinly disguised Slavophile. His 'was a programme of undiluted revolution, political, social, and national. It would dethrone kings and emperors, destroy the power and riches of the bourgeoisies, dissolve the unnatural conglomeration of races known as the Austrian Empire and, through the liberation of the Slav peoples, pave the way for a European federation of free republics. These dreams were completed by another—the dream of the Russian revolution, thought of sometimes as the starting-point, sometimes. as the culmination of the universal revolution, but always as its crown and quintessence.[112]

In its essentials not much different is the case of Prince P. A. Kropotkin, who sought a scientific foundation for anarchist theory and was an enlightened and pacified Bakunin.

We find the same combination of a 'humanistic fog', strong ethical bent, sentimental populism, and sometimes political reformism but always social revolutionarism, in the essential economic and social thought of all non-Marxian revolutionary parties in Russia since the middle of the 19th century. There is the same ethical foundation for socialism, and not one of historical materialism; the same messianism, the same stress on a different way of introducing socialism in Russia, as the country did not yet possess a bourgeoisie but conserved its precious institutions of mir and artel. An economic interpretation of this belief as an 'ideology of natural economy', introduced by Peter Struve and so fashionable in the nineties of the 19th century, does not seem to give a complete and satisfactory explanation.

The entire group of Russian agrarian socialism, including the *Narodnaya Volya*, Narodniki, and the party of Social revolutionaries, in spite of all their theoretical distinctions and different methods had one thing in common: for all of them Russian capitalism was a 'bastard of history'. The type of religious crusade of 'going into the People' started in the eighties by the Narodniki who followed them, the philisophizing deliberations of the subjectivists. even the Social Revolutionary party—all of them idolized the Russian muzhik; all of them were much nearer to the Slavophiles than they realized. The muzhik play for this group the same role as the proletariat in the structure of orthodox Marxism. It was an echo of old Rousseauism. In all these teachings one can hear Rousseau's words: 'It is the village which makes the country, and

[112] Carr, *op. cit.,* p. 80.

85

the rural people who make the nation.' It was possibly a belated echo of physiocracy—a current which previously had been almost without effect on Russian thought. Contact with the muzhik was thought of not only as a social service but as a chance to acquire from the common people its ethical ideas and its wisdom. One can trace here the religious roots of Russian atheism.

The situation is now clear. All groups, including the orthodox Marxian Social Democrats, resented economic liberalism; but in distinction from the orthodox Social Democrats most of them saw no necessity for Russia to pass through the mill of capitalism, thanks to the peculiarities of Russian development. Thus only the orthodox Social Democrats remained uncompromising Westerners; otherwise it was a tacit revival, a silent regeneration of the Slavophile current which the left wing of the Russian intelligentsia adopted in the last quarter of the 19th century.

Knowingly or unknowingly, willingly or unwillingly all these groups of thought became permeated by a revived economic nativism. It is irrelevant for our purposes to analyse the details of the teachings of the leading Populists like V. V. (Vorontsov)[113] or Nicolai-on (Danielson).[114] Like their predecessors and their followers, they have in common admiration for Russian past; belief in the advent of socialism in Europe; and as immediate purpose, elimination of capitalism, which had been, in their opinion, compulsorily imported into Russia. They resented the revolutionary Marxism of Plekhanov not less than the evolutionary Marxism of Struve.

Berdyayev is correct in his statement that 'the Marxists considered the 'narodniks' reactionaries who supported obsolete forms of economics. The 'narodniks' regarded the Marxists as supporters of capitalism and bound to contribute to its developments."[115]

The Social Revolutionary party inherited most of the features of Narodnaya Volya and of the Narodniki. It differed from the first by emphasis on socialism, and from the others, whose immediate heir it was, by some Marxian colouring. But, to the 'S.R.', as to their predecessors, the peasant was the centre of the development; peculiarly Russian ways of development toward socialism were axiomatic for them.

The so-called subjective-sociological school with its belief in the 'critically thinking individual' as the centre of progress goes back, really, to Pisarev's 'thinking realists'. P. L. Lavrov (Mirtov), an

[113] V. V., *The Destiny of Capitalism in Russia*, St. Petersburg, 1882.
[114] Nicolai-on, *Sketches of our Public Economy after the Reforms*, St. Petersburg, 1893.
[115] Berdyayev, *op. cit.*, p. 120.

artillery officer, who originated the current in his *Historical Letters,* resented historical materialism and preached ethical socialism. Lavrov's follower was N. K. Mikhailovski, who exercised a great influence on the young generation, and whose monthly review *Russian Wealth* was read and studied as if it were Scripture all over Russia.

Mikhailovski signifies the final split of Russian socialist thought into two camps—that of Marxian labour and that of national agrarian Populism, the latter appearing in different clothes and disguises. Opposing economic liberalism, as well as Marxian socialism, Mikhailovski expressed some sympathy toward the German ethical school and toward *Kathedersozialismus.*

Like Lavrov, Mikhailovski believed in the strength and importance of critically-minded personalities in addition to the importance of peculiar Russian institutions. He claimed that the radical intelligentsia, utilizing the lessons of the West and applying advanced science, would be able to deprive Russia of the horror and misery of the transitional bourgeois age. But he admitted that this possibility was dwindling daily. Mikhailovski hoped the government would take the initiative in introducing the new social structure.

This school had numerous followers, such as the economist S. N. Yuzhakov, the historian N. I. Kareyev, the publicist A. V. Peshekonov, the statistician N. F. Annenski, and others. All of them preached in tune with the Populists, all of them were in favour of governmental intervention, all of them opposed official Marxism, all of them introduced in their teachings seeds of nationalism and anti-Westernism.

The climax of the Russian reaction against Western ideas was represented by the great trio of predecessors of Oswald Spengler: N. Y. Danilevski, Konstantin Leontyev, and Vladimir Solovyov.

Herzen observed once that the significant feature of his period was *grübeln.* This group of Russian thinkers practised *grübeln* in a grand style and on a large scale, and was full of *Weltschmerz* and messianism.

Danilevski—a scientist and statistician by education and profession, a student of ichthyology who made outstanding contributions to Russian legislation on fisheries—early became interested in social questions. He was a member of the Petrashevski circle. Danilevski wrote on psychological, economic, and political topics. His articles in *Zarya* (1869) appeared in 1871 in book form under the title *Russia and Europe,* and presented his theory of cultural-historical types. Danilevski's great book practically originated in anti-Germanism. It begins with the statement 'that an event of immense historical importance occurred in the summer of 1866. Germany, split during centuries, began to integrate under the guidance of the brilliant Prussian Minister, integrate into one strong unit. The European *status quo* was obviously disrupted'.

The broad picture of the last pages of his famous book gives a good understanding of Danilevski's trend of thought. The mainstream of world history begins, according to Danilevski, with two sources on the banks of the ancient Nile. One, the divine, the celestial, via Jerusalem and Constantinople, reaches in its original purity Kiev and Moscow; the other, human and earthy, is split into two main channels: culture and politics; it passes Athens, Alexandria, Rome on the way to the countries of Europe; it dries up sometimes, but is enriched again by new abundant side-streams. A new source is breaking out on Russian soil—the trend of a just social-economic structure safeguarding the masses of population. Russia is, in Danilevski's conception, a compact unit not having any colonies or possessions but spreading and extending itself on all its borders. This gigantic country is in a position distinct from Europe in regard to planning its future. In the West there are many plans but no material for reconstruction; Russia possesses the material. The Russian development shows many important distinctions from the West. First of all is the matter of incentive. Private interest has never been and is not the driving motive of the Russians. Inasmuch as interest is the basis of any party organization, the Russian system differs from the West European or Roman-German. The other Russian peculiarity is the tempo of development. When the Russian people decides on a change and starts an action, the transformation takes place with an unusual speed and seemingly without too much opposition. Imitation of Europe is a Russian disease, Danilevski explained in Chapter XI of his book. Peter the Great's reforms should have been cultivated from the inside and not planted from above, and Russian life should not become compulsorily Europeanized.

Danilevski's attack on Europe is violent. 'Such a thing as Europe does not exist at all; it is just the Western peninsula of Asia' (p. 58). The question 'Is the West rotting?' receives an affirmative answer in Chapter VII, which sounds like Oswald Spengler's *Decline of the West;*[116] Europe does not regard Russia as belonging to it (p. 50); a fight with Europe is unavoidable, as 'Russia is too great

[116] It is interesting to note that the anti-Western, anti-German ideas of the Russians, often influenced by German philosophy and inspired by German sources, in the 20th century exercised a boomerang influence on the German intelligentsia in its conception of the decline of the West.

and powerful to be just one of the Great European Powers' (p. 435).

There must be, says Danilevski, a generally Slav federation without Poland, but including Greeks, Rumanians, and Hungarians, 'whose historical destinies have attached them by indestructible bonds to the Slav world'. There must be a war between Slavism and Europe which will fill a whole period of history: and Constantinople must be won: but it must not be the capital of Russia because Moscow is the centre of his visions.

K. N. Leontyev belonged to the same current of thought. By profession a surgeon; diplomat, editor of a military newspaper, censor, novelist, philosopher—he ended his life in a monastery. The ideals of this ultraconservative were to preserve the mystic Byzantine Christianity, strong and centralized monarchial government and the original beauty and simplicity of life in its national forms. Here we see clearly the triad: Orthodoxy, Absolutism and Populism. Leontyev's theory of social revolution was influenced by Saint-Simon, Hegel, Auguste Comte, and Herbert Spencer although he himself disclaimed any previous knowledge of Spencer, Leontyev warned against democratization and equalization of Russia as a result of Europeanization. He suggests 'preservation of barbarism' as the only way to save Russia and make it great.

The violence of Danilevski's thought and the intolerance of Leontyev are in contrast with the philosophical speculations, dreams of great vision, and deep personal sincerity of V. S. Solovyov, the son of the historian S. M. Solovyov, and one of the founders of Russian philosophy. We find in Solovyov's writing the same negation of the West (Crises of Western Philosophy, Moscow, 1874) and Slavophilism (which he soon discarded); the same religious search, which resulted in his conversion to Roman Catholicism in 1896; dreams of a united Catholic church headed by the Pope and the Tsar; and prophecies of the advent of anti-Christ and the destruction of Western civilization by Mongols headed by Japan. His famous Three Conversations (published in the Week) dealing with war, progress, and the end of world history, present the climax of Solovyov's thought and fears. Solovyov's well-known Pan-Mongolism reveals his vision of another direction of Russian history:

> Pan-Mongolism! though the word is strange
> My ear acclaims its gongs.

Solovyov's conversion to Catholicism was in the old tradition of the Russian intelligentsia. The religious supranational messianic ideas of Russian thought, its anti-individualism, its total global outlook, found an outlet and reaction in the conversion to Catholicism, which could be considered in many cases as an expression of national supranationalism. Sir John Maynard was one of the first to emphasize this feature, but without giving it a plausible explanation.[117]

The 20th century witnessed two revivals of Russian nativism: one at the height of the tsarist empire's power, the other in the gloomy exile in Europe. It was in Moscow, prior to the First World War, that the neo-Slavophiles began the concentration of their forces under the leadership of Prince Eugene Trubetskoi and his *Moscow Weekly*. Representatives of several political parties participated in the collection of essays under the title *Great Russia*,[118] which was a kind of manifesto of the new Russian nationalism. P. B. Struve formulated in the second issue (1911) the 'Economic Problem of Great Russia'. Symbolically, the publisher and editor of this collection was the multi-millionaire V. P. Ryabushinsky, a representative of the native bourgeoisie looking for political influence and leadership in Russia's domestic policies, who sought to make Russia a powerful influence in world politics.

The old trend of anti-Westernism and Slavophilism had another revival after World War I, in exile, but under the influence of the revolution of 1917. The *Eurasian* teachings proclaimed by Russian emigrants in Prague, headed by Prince N. S. Trubetskoi and N. P. Savitski, regard European culture as the real enemy of Russia, and acclaim the Bolshevism which led to Russia's withdrawal from the European type of life. But while the Bolsheviks declared

---

[117] ". . . More than one Russian religious thinker has found virtues in Catholicism, to the loss of which he has attributed some of Russia's failings." *Russia in Flux*, p. 159. Mysticism and religious searching often appeared in Russia as a reaction against liberal ideas. That was the case of Alexander I, of the Slavophiles, and of Catholicism. The philosophy of the free thinkers and Voltairians of the end of the 18th century and beginning of the 19th century was replaced by a brief episode of Catholic domination and a more influential spread of mysticism. The Jesuits exercised their influence on the feminine part of the aristocracy of St Petersburg; they established their institute in the capital, a school in Odessa, and so on, but were expelled from Russia in 1822. The teachings of English Quakers, headed by Julia Krudener and Tatarinova, came in vogue, as well as a revival of Masonism. Influence of Lamennais' Catholic socialist doctrines was vividly felt in the thirties of the 19th century. The case of the Decembrist Lunin's conversion is well known. More important was the case of Professor Vladimir Pecherin, whose disappointments in Western socialism led him to Catholicism; he became a Redemptorist stationed in Ireland. The Catholic sympathies of Chaadayev and Gogol are well known.

[118] *Great Russia, Collection of Essays on Military and Social Problems,* Book I, Moscow, 1910.

war on the bourgeois civilization of Europe, the Eurasians resented the German-Roman civilization of Europe. At the same time many of the school remind one vividly of their German sources, as, for instance, the Savitski doctrine contrasting 'the Mongol *feeling* of the continent with the West European *feeling* of the sea'. Eurasians in their withdrawal from Europe could be characterized as neo-Slavophiles looking to Asia more than to the European Slavic elements. They shared Pushkin's complaint that 'Europe has always been ignorant of and ungrateful to Russia'.

# VI. Reaction and Synthesis : Bolshevism

Hail ! Young, unknown people!
PUSHKIN.

You are the same as you were and not
the same,
You turned to me your new face
And a new vision troubles me.
BLOK.

**A**LL world waves of economic ideas reached and affected Russian thought. The older Western national cultures, such as the English and French, had their brief hours of success and influence in Russia; isolated representatives of other nations, like the Spaniard Jovellanos or the North American Alexander Hamilton, were occasionally studied and admired by the Russian intelligentsia. But German influence, as we observed in the previous chapters, became dominant and victorious on the threshold of the 19th and the 20th centuries. As a result of geographical, historic, and economic factors German economics of all colourings, with their philosophical foundations, permeated the Russian mind. It is true that in many cases the Germans in turn were affected and influenced in their ideas by Russian actual conditions: but the rise of the German Empire, the growth of her economic power, and her deliberate policy of penetrating the Eastern empire resulted in a complete domination of Russian economic thought. The nascent Russian bourgeoisie received its inspiration from Friedrich List, and superficially and rather late from the German historical school: the restless and ever searching intelligentsia, first in love with Schelling, fluctuated between, or tried to reconcile, Hegel and Kant, the native currents and the political right wing, especially the more mystic Slavophiles and chauvinist Pan-Slavists, influenced by German teachings, played with the conception of the 'Russian soul'; on the left wing were ardent disciples of Karl Marx, and even the dissenters followed the paths of German revisionism and German idealism; and, of course, Lasalle's and Bismarck's state socialism had not left Russian thought and practice untouched.

For some time German theories were welcome ammunition in Russians' defence against the penetration of Western capitalism with its prevailing insular English classical ideas. A continent in

92

itself, not unlike the United States, Russia, a late-comer on the scene of technological advancement, resented the self-contented concept of the anti-historical economists who considered their theoretical manipulations valid *semper ubique*. Symbolically, for the Slavophiles, a 'European' was always an Englishman.

Of course, German ideas acquired different colourings on Russian soil. The Russians added to German romanticism a constant restlessness, perpetual discontent, and untiring search for justice and perfection; they injected a strong dose of idealism into German materialism; they expanded German theories and programmes, often depriving them of their orderliness and symmetry, and developed them on a global scale. A reaction against German domination of Russian economic thought was inevitable.

Ernest J. Simmons aptly observed that 'throughout the whole history of Russia there were periodic awakenings, sudden reversions to the national 'idea' and culture during which Russia struggled against the engulfing waves of foreign ascendancy.'[119] On the other hand, a unifying national thought was needed in order to digest the century-old receptions from abroad, revise, adjust and apply them to Russian conditions.

Increasingly conflicting developments clashed early in the 20th century: Russia's efforts fully to develop its productive forces and Germany's efforts to stop or control this development. Germany constantly tried to use financial means for this purpose. Thus in 1887 Bismarck gave official support to a campaign against Russian credit, and until 1894 the German market remained closed to Russian governmental securities. In 1893-94 and 1903-04 tariff disputes clouded the relations. In 1911 in connection with the Agadir incident Germany used financial pressure on Russia, suddenly withdrawing short-term credits. The general trend of German foreign policy changed, as we know, after Bismarck's fall.

Russia endeavoured to tie up its future with the non-German world. Hence the French-Russian alliance, the Triple Entente; hence the preference given to French and British capital in an attempt to liberate the country's economy from Germans and German capital. I described this process on the eve of World War I in my *German Capital in Russia*.[120]

Russia's raw materials required world markets and not German intermediaries; Russia's desire was to import machinery and not

---

119 Simmons, *op. cit.*, p. 3.
120 *German Capital in Russia*, 1st ed., St. Petersburg, 1914; 2nd ed., Petrograd, 1918.

German manufactured goods. New ways and new means had to be found to materialize and accelerate the process of Russian economic emancipation. New ideas were necessary.

In a nutshell the situation was as follows: In order to be politically independent, in order to preserve its national culture, Russia had to be technologically and economically strong. That was obvious to all Russian reformers, Peter the Great being the best example. The great Russian historian S. Solovyov emphasized it: 'First of all in order to overcome our economic bankruptcy it was necessary to get richer and stronger'.[121]

It is true that Russia prior to 1917 was in possession of some industrialized regions highly concentrated geographically and dominated by few big units with up-to-date machinery. It was mainly a case of heavy industry, producing railway equipment and armaments. It was mainly a case of St. Petersburg, Moscow, and Kharkov, which became at the same time the concentration places and vanguard of the Russian proletariat. But, for instance, agricultural machinery and corrugated iron had to be imported.

The old tempo of industrialization, while rapid since the end of the 19th century, was not sufficient to catch up with and overtake the more advanced West, to provide for Russia's security and the possibility of unhindered development of its resources, to prevent Russia from remaining a German hinterland and becoming a German colony.

The traditionless Russian capitalism, which was almost as recent as a Victorian sofa, did not fulfil this function. It was too young, not strongly enough developed, did not have a sufficiently broad social basis to obtain complete political power and control its own destiny. The climate of liberal individualism was strange to Russian history, and etatistic ideas were familiar. The unfinished agrarian reform of 1861, which, as in Prussia, left a system of big land estates, was another obstacle to the formation of a large national domestic market, and slowed up the proletarization of the peasantry. Stolypin's attempt to establish a class of peasant landowners started too late. The growth of a middle class was hindered as the Russian bourgeoisie had to labour under pressures from remainders of feudalism, above, and a growing labour movement below. Obviously none of the old ruling classes could solve the problem of the early 20th century in Russia.

Meanwhile new technological achievements made possible short cuts in economic development; symptoms of abandonment of undiluted liberal individualism became noticeable on a world scale,

[121] S. Solovyov, *History of Russia*, Part 2, p. 805.

regimentation and planning in the World War I period strengthened this trend.

If liberal. capitalism failed its mission in Russia, what were the economic forms which could secure the full development of Russia's potential economic strength under the real conditions and circumstances of the post-World War I period?

Now, more than a quarter of a century after the Russian Revolution, we can see that its economic motive was the necessity to fight, not primarily Western capitalism as a whole, but its nearest and most dangerous position: German penetration. Even using German assistance and co-operation in the troublesome years between two world wars, even complaining about capitalist intervention and new encirclement attempts, the actual work of the Soviet regime, concentrated around fast and complete industrialization of Russia, was directed first and most of all against the dangerous, scheming neighbour in the West.

The revolt against German economic penetration was followed by a parallel revolt against German domination in the field of economic thought, a revolt against the teachings and tactics of the German Social Democratic party. History seldom witnessed more bitter factional fights than that of the Bolsheviks against the 'social traitors', against theoreticians like Kautsky, politicians like Noske and Scheidemann, to cite just a few examples.

This anti-German tendency of the Bolsheviks was not new; it was rather traditional in Russian history.

Early Russian mercantilists; Decembrists, Herzen and his generation of socialist thinkers; the anarchist Bakunin; great writers and poets like Lermontov, Saltykov-Shchedrin, Turgenev, Tolstoy and up to Mayakovski, were full of hatred towards Germany.

Krizânic insisted that it 'is time to throw out all Germans'; Pososhkov complained that the Germans 'bring poverty to us and enrich themselves at our expense'. Fonvizin wrote from Germany: 'Everything is better in our country, and we are more *men* than the Germans', Ryleyev's letter from Paris in 1814 is known; he accused the Prussians of cruelty in their attitude toward the French civil population.

Even the inception of the Decembrists' organization was partly caused by the resentment against German influence.[122]

For Bakunin, the German was the eternal oppressor of the Slav. Herzen stated that 'The hostility between Slavs and Germans is a

---

[122] Hessen, *The Decembrists Before the Court of History*, Leningrad, 1925, p. 28.

sad but recognized fact. Each conflict between them reveals the depth of their hatred'.

Saltykov-Shchedrin (a member of the Petrashevski group) in his *Abroad* declared: 'Berlin exists for murder only'; in his *Complicated Affair* he created the immortal type of a German-Russian socialist, 'Wolfgang Antonovich Beobachter, cand. phil'. One of Shchedrin's heroes addresses the following speech to a German: 'Who is the worst oppressor of the Russian worker?—The German. Who is the most pitiless pedagogue in Russia?—The German. Who is the most cruel administrator?—The German'. Gleb Uspenski, who visited Berlin at the same period as Saltykov-Shchedrin, described in his letters the repulsive militarism of Germany victorious over France. General R. Fadeyev, in his influential *Opinion on the Eastern Question,* declared that 'our chief enemy is not Western Europe but the German tribe with its limitless ambitions.[123] Katkov's anti-German campaign was violent and influential. Lermontov, Gogol, Nekrasov, Turgenev, Dostoyevski—all the great of Russian literature—painted devastating pictures of Germans in Russia. While the Russian Mensheviks were, generally speaking, captives of the German influence, their leader Plekhanov resented German ambitions for the role of teachers of Russia.[124]

Eugene Tarlé, who is, one could say, the contemporary official Soviet historian, generalizes this idea on behalf of Soviet historians: 'Long before Hitler, a tradition existed in Germany which aimed at the annihilation of Russia. Generations were brought up in hate and contempt for Russia even when Hitler had never been heard of. But nothing of this was said by our historians, and our graduates did not know the danger which threatened our country'.[125] The anti-German renaming of St. Petersburg into Petrograd was symbolically continued by the Bolsheviks and only later changed to Leningrad after 1917. The Russian purges of technicians, of old Bolsheviks, of generals, used always to take the form of a fight against pro-German elements.

In my understanding, the Bolshevik revolution was the expression of an organic and not an outside revolt; it was the inevitable result of the one-and-a-half centuries-long history of the Russian intelligentsia, prepared by the Russian past and imperative for its

---

[123] R. Fadeyev, *Opinion on the Eastern Question,* St. Petersburg, 1870, p. 86.

[124] Cf. P. Judin in his article on the twenty-fifth anniversary of G. V. Plekhanov's death; *Bolshevik,* May, 1943 (No. 10).

[125] Eugene Tarlé, " Soviet Historical Research," *Science and Society,* Summer, 1943, p. 231.

future. It was a reaction against and prevention of continued German hegemony in Russian economic life and thought.

It started as a revolution against Western capitalist forms and against German socialism—itself a product of Western capitalist structure. But the shadow of Slavophile teachings still lay heavy on Russian thought. Russian economic thought has always been a dream poem; in its positive part, fighting the classic dragon of capitalism; in its negative part, revolting against the romanticism of man's eternal unfulfilment. But dreams themselves can be at times only too realistic.

In this combination of romantic epic and sober realism lies the world historical importance of 1917. Masaryk was right in stating that the 'problem of revolution was a Russian revolution'.[126]

And, again, looking a quarter of a century back, I believe not only that the Bolshevist revolution was inevitable but also that it was more along Russian traditions than its contemporaries realized. I disagree with the conception of Russians abroad that the revolution of 1917 was an incident, a tragedy, a catastrophe.

The Russian 'white' emigration in its personal sorrow did not comply with the dictum of the Chinese poet:[127]

> When you must go—then go
> And make as little fuss as you can.

Contemporaries forgot that for centuries the spectre of revolution had loomed on the Russian horizon, that one hundred years of the history of the Russian intelligentsia was the seedtime, that the revolution of 1917 led to a solution of 'Russia the Sphinx'; that the years of war communism and civil war were just an episode in Russian history. The fundamental aims and aspirations of the Soviet Union have their deep roots in Russian history.

Time had to pass in order to enable a *post factum* diagnosis of such a great controversial phenomenon as the revolution of 1917. The understanding was coming to our minds slowly and unconsciously. World War II brought the subterranean process to the surface. I agree with Sir John Maynard that 'Russia is in flux; but it is the same Russia though with a new and important psychological addition made by the "evolution".'

Penetration of the intellectual climate of the twenty-five years since the revolution is more important for the understanding of modern Russia than a most painstaking study of the theory of communism and its interpretation and application in the Soviet

[126] Masaryk, *op. cit.*, Vol. II, p. 480.
[127] Tao Chien, (A.D 365-427).

G

Union. In its loves and hatreds, dreams and recollections, hopes and disappointments, in word and in deed, the Russian Revolution is a natural and logical continuation of Russian traditions. It became crystallized as a result of the great schisms of the forties between the Westerners and Slavophiles, in the nineties between the Populists and Marxists, in 1903 between the Bolsheviks and Mensheviks, in the thirties of the 20th century between the Stalinists and Trotzkyites.

Our methods of examination will be changed now. In the study of foreign influences and native currents we have had to rely mostly, if not exclusively, on statements made by Russian writers and statesmen, economists and political scientists. We cannot use the same method in an examination of the Soviet trends. The characteristic of the post-revolution period in Russia was action and not theorizing, and even theoretical changes took place by way of actions—in some cases later acknowledged by theoretical pronunciamentos. There was certainly a period of discussions and arguments. Internal factional battles like that of Trotzkyism had their theoretical clothes. And there were continuous fights against heresies. There were periods of exaggerations, of stubborn dogmatism; but the economic conditions required not theorizing but action, not abstract sophistications of planning, but planning itself; the problems became no longer a matter of theory but of practice, of self-preservation, of daily bread even without butter, of national existence and independence. The entire character of Russian economics changed.

In the first years after the revolution, pre-revolutionary professors attempted to smuggle in and publish their belated dissertations. The study of business cycles was continued. N. D. Kondratyev developed his theory of long waves; others studied problems of banking and currency; L. N. Yurovski got involved in the theory of prices. There was a group of theoretically inclined 'old' Bolsheviks headed by Bukharin, Preobrazhenski, Strumilin, with others. But since in the Soviet Union the state and economy became one, and the idea of central planning was put in operation, economics necessarily took on a different aspect and developed into an administrative art. Search for 'blue distance' and Herzen's *grübeln* were replaced by collection of facts for action, discussions of methods of action, and actions themselves. This development is not peculiar to the Soviet Union but typical of any state-managed economy. Bureaucratization of economic life results in bureaucratization of economics. It is a marked trend towards *neocameralia*.

The Bolsheviks showed themselves elastic enough to escape

the 'sickness of leftism', as Lenin dubbed it; to realize that socialism is not uniform *semper ubique* but adopts local colourings and is subject to historical changes. In this way, rather unconsciously, the inheritance of the Russian past, of the Russian intelligentsia, became adjusted, under changed and changing conditions, to the ruling *Weltanschauung*. Apostles of revolution became high officials, leaders of the economic life. After a brief period of fractional fights the new style of Russian economics moved decidedly toward problems of application. The purpose, method, and spirit of Russian economics changed as a result of the collectivist, planned character of the economy. The Russians are developing a new style that might be called 'constructional economics'.

The real school of economics in Russia is, of course, the Gosplan with all its numerous branches and sections.

The new Soviet bureaucracy covered the country with a mass of special research institutes, established numerous economic periodicals, expanded the statistical output. 'Applied economics' became the centre of studies, with economic geography (as the foundation of theory of location) in special vogue. One has to be acquainted with the Soviet periodical economic literature to realize the intensity and thoroughness of their empirical investigations of domestic and international problems.[128]

Dealing in their daily life with concrete economic problems and not with abstract theorems, the Russians were confronted with actual conditions of time and place formed as a result of a centuries-long process. In this way they had unconsciously to resume the thread of traditionalism which the episode of war communism broke up. I am going to prove this contention by way of parallels between some basic conceptions in the so-called Old and New Russia. Obviously my attempt is not exhaustive and should serve only as illustration. But the constant, striking parallelism is in itself an affirmation and proof.

What strikes an observer first and strongest is the organic and integral understanding of economy and economic society in the Soviet Union, in reference to their country as well as to the entire globe. The indivisibility of the world under present technological conditions is an axiom for the Soviets (an axiom on which they base their international policy). But we saw how the Slavophiles, how, for instance, Chernyshevski, long before the Bolsheviks,

[128] An interesting picture (although not correct in regard to the period prior to 1917 and too sketchy for the period since 1917) of " Economic Education and Economic Research in the Soviet Union " is presented by J. Zvavich in *The Economic Journal*, London, December, 1943, pp. 415-418.

opposed the English classical thinkers and stressed the necessity for observing society as a whole. One could seldom find in Russian economics representative of the atomistic view.

Bolshevism remained faithful to Russian tradition in its ethical content and emphasis, and regards itself as the answer to the traditional Russian search for universal social justice. P. N. Sakulin, in his *Russian Literature and Socialism*, emphasized that the entire dynamics of the historical process of Russia at least in the last one hundred years 'was directed to one aim—to abolish social injustice, to transform the unjust culture, the culture of the privileged minority, into a structure corresponding to the interests of working masses'.[129] The Russian had not identified himself with a Western European, but with a member of humanity. All mankind! Eternity! have always been Russian slogans.

The great Russian literature adopted a prophetic character in its alarm at impending catastrophe. In unison with Russian economists it claimed (or foresaw?) that the entire world, Russia included, was hanging over an abyss and falling into it. Hence the permanent intellectual unrest in Russian minds, their constant search for the salvation of mankind.[130] Hence the Russian messianism. 'The Russian mission is indisputably European and universal. To become a real Russian, to become entirely Russian, perhaps only means to become the brother of all men, an all-man.' (Dostoyevski's Speech on Pushkin's Anniversary, June 8, 1880).

And again this trend finds its unofficial rebirth after the revolution. Karl Nötzel observed at the end of the old regime that it is the old 'claim that the way to all-mankind necessarily leads through the all-Russian';[131] and the head and dean of Soviet literature a quarter of a century later declares: 'the moral and historic meaning for all humanity of all Soviet construction, the unique path for the development of society, was the innovation which Soviet literature brought in the treasure house of the world's literature'.[132] The combination of love for 'the cast down and reviled' and belief in Russia's reforming the world can be felt under the surface of the Bolshevik climate not less than in the writings of Tolstoy and Dostoyevski and in the self-sacrificing fight of

[129] P. N. Sakulin, *Russian Literature and Socialism,* Moscow, 1922, Vol. 1, p. 6.

[130] Messianism was not strange to the young Marx: he declared that " the emancipation of Germany means the emancipation of mankind." " Criticism of Hegel's Philosophy of Law " (appeared in *Deutsch-Französische Jahrbücher* in 1844).

[131] Karl Nötzel, *Die Grundlage des geistigen Russlands,* Jena, 1917, p. 1.

[132] Alexey Tolstoy, " Trends in Soviet Literature," *Science and Society,* Summer, 1943, p. 234.

early revolutionaries. The entire history of Russia is full of messianic beliefs—religious, political, social. *The Book of Degrees* of the middle of the 16th century formulated one of the first philosophies of Russian history as that of an Orthodox empire, presenting the Russian people as unique and exclusive, born to perform a world mission.

The idea of an Orthodox world empire became, for a long period, the Russian central idea. Russian Slavophilism saw a conjunction of the national moment with the universal world historical one, as Schelling's philosophy of history required.[133]

Sceptic and pessimist, the Westerner Chaadayev, terrified by the Russian actuality, believed that 'it is our destiny to solve most of the problems of social order, fulfil most of the ideas originated in old societies'; he loved his fatherland 'for its future only'. The Slavophile Pogodin was satisfied that 'the political fate of Europe and consequently the fate of the world is in our hands if we desire to solve it'. Pogodin predicted the end of the bourgeois rule in Europe under the pressure of the proletariat, while in Russia he expected the same results to be achieved through the wise policy of the tsarist government.

From contemplating the special characteristics of the Slavic world, Danilevski, as we know already, arrived at the conclusion that the 'Slavic historical type of culture will for the first time present a synthesis of all the aspects of cultural activity'.

Sometimes the religious, political, and economic messianism was expressed in strange visions like those of K. Leontyev, who dreamed of a monarchial reactionary socialism of the Russian tsar in Constantinople, assisted by a revolutionary labour movement in the West and in Russia. Russian Fourierists, like the Petrashevski circle, Russian anarchists headed by Bakunin, and, of course, the whole of Russian literature—all expressed belief in the great mission of Russia. Slavophiles and Westerners, Populists and revisionists, reactionaries and radicals, the 'Black Hundred' and the revolutionaries—all classes, groups, currents, sooner or later became victims to the spell of Russia's world mission, including, of course, the mystical believers in the 'God-bearing people', the later Eurasians, and not excluding the Social Revolutionaries. Typically, militant Westerners often changed their 'landmarks' and joined the believers in a peculiarly Russian mission in world

---

[133] In a remarkable footnote I. Kireyevski considered just two nations of the world—Russia and the United States—as favourably distinct from declining Europe; but he placed all his hopes on Russia. (*Works,* edited by Gershenson, Vol. II, pp. 38-39). Pecherin, too, saw Russia and the United States as beginning a new cycle of history.

history. They felt that even if the European flowers were the best, most beautiful, and last word of civilization, yet Russian soil still contained promising seeds of its wild herbs, and not merely thistles. The only group which remained free from this spell were the Russian Mensheviks.[134]

The Soviet Union followed this messianic complex. Internationalism became conceived as a national Russian idea. The 'International' became the national anthem. The Third Rome of the Slavophiles was replaced by the Third International. Russia the prophet, the world saviour, the world leader was the belief and subconscious guiding thought of the revolution of 1917. The militant liberating mission of the world proletariat became the Russian mission. The messianism of the world proletariat became identified with that of Russia. It developed in Soviet practice into an organic synthesis of old Russian notions and communist teachings. The Soviet practice unconsciously made use of some Russian irrational elements which became organically combined with the official teachings of Marxian rationalism. It was an inheritance of the Russian maximalism so full of messianic mystic visions.

The idea of the proletariat—the messiah, the victor, the world organizer—militant, aggressive, dominating, the bearer of the final truth and justice, found fruitful soil. It was at the same time a contrast and protest against the passive, old, suffering elements of some Russian currents of the Tolstoy type. The eternal rebel became victorious over the docile, passive type of Russian.

Mayakovski expressed this universal messianism in his *Mystery-Bouffe* when he dreamed of attack against distant planets and showed at the end the promised land of the industrialized earth. Mayakovski's messianism in this mystery embraced the universe; at the beginning of the revolution he wanted to unite *only* all workers, eliminating 'all others'. Internationalism was Russian nationalism at the beginning of the revolution; it appeared as the national Russian vocation. After the decision on the course of 'socialism in a single country' was taken, nationalism became Russian internationalism in the Second World War.

The new Russian thought developed a new messianism by example of achievements of the Soviet Union.[135] The French

---

[134] One of the few Western socialists who felt the existence of a special kind of Russian socialism and of a national Russian way toward socialism was Otto Bauer in his pamphlet *Die Russische Revolution und das Europäische Proletariat*, Vienna, 1917 (under the pseudonym Heinrich Weber), and later on in his *Rationalisierung und Fehl Rationalisierung*, Vienna, 1931.

[135] Cavour expressed the same trend of thought. He wrote to a Russian

Revolution with its ideals of internationalism brought nationalism into being. The foreign menace moved France to the first great burst of national enthusiasm in the modern sense. The new national enthusiasm supplied France with soldiers so numerous and so spirited that she not only repelled her invaders but began to invade other countries in turn, theoretically on a mission of emancipation, but leading to Napoleon and imperialist aggression. Looking back we can see two faces of the revolution of 1917, the international and national, and a comparison with the French revolution is in place. The French Revolution defended New France against feudal Europe, and Soviet Russia defended New Russia against the bourgeois West. The French Revolution was compelled to defend the idea of revolution against reactionary Europe, and the revolutionary army of France exclaimed at Valmy, *'Vive la Nation!'* Enthusiasm in defending the conquests of the revolution against European reaction strengthened the national element in the international character of Russian nationalism.[136]

The Russian mission in history will be achieved by specifically Russian ways of economic development—the Populist V. V. expressed this common belief of the Russian intelligentsia in stating that 'Russian capitalism is history's illegitimate child'. As we have seen, Decembrists, Slavophiles, Westerners (Herzen! Belinski!), Populists, Social Revolutionaries, practically all Russian parties and factions, with exception of the Mensheviks, and almost the entire Russian literature, even with such contrasts as Pushkin and Dostoyevski, from different standpoints and for different reasons, preached Russia's escaping the capitalist age. German scholars like Herder, Schlözer, Haxthausen, Roscher felt the same way. Schelling touched upon this idea. The Russians always saw themselves in the role of a Vulcan who had forged a key to unlock the mysteries of social development. The economic cosmos in their opinion was becoming an outflowing of the human spirit. The advance of technique made this possible, and for this reason the premature birth of Russian socialism was not a miscarriage.

The Bolsheviks of the Stalin period adopted a quite similar interpretation of Marx and Engels. In their fight with Trotskyism

---

diplomat: "What will make your country master of Europe later on is not its armies but its communal organization."

136 The Russian poet F. Tyutchev, with his peculiar mysticism, made the following statement in a not well-known letter after the Crimean War: "If the West would be united, it seems that we would have to perish. But there are two in the West: the *Red* and the one whom the *Red* has to absorb. For forty years we defended this booty from the *Red*, but we are on the edge of the abyss and it is now precisely that the *Red* will save us."

and insistence on socialism in a single country they emphasized that the 'teachings of the founders of Marxism of the possibility of escaping and shortening the capitalist stage of development in backward countries became a reality and not merely a possibility in the U.S.S.R.'[137] From this standpoint they resent the accusation that Russian development violates logic by the fact of the sudden jump of an industrially unripe country into socialism. They claim that the jump is logically consistent with Marxian teachings, and that 'Marx and Engels and not the revolutionary Populists supplied the scientific foundation for non-capitalist methods of developing backward countries. This theory, under different historical conditions, was developed and elaborated by Lenin and Stalin.'[138]

Here lies the foundation of the theoretical clash between Stalinism and Trotzkyism. Against Trotzkyism's insistence on the necessity of passing through the stages known from Western history, Stalinism follows the line of specifically Russian ways of development. Both claim to be the only correct interpretation of Marx and Engels.

[137] N. Berro, " K. Marx and F. Engels on Non-Capitalist Development of Backward Countries," *Revolutionary East*, No. 3-4, 1933, p. 25.

[138] From an article by N. Berro (see reference 13, p. 161). A recent American study supports this view. " These stages do not appear outside of the West in anything like the prescribed order. Of this fact Marx himself was clearly aware. He expected India to pass from communalism to capitalism, leaving out feudalism and perhaps also another stage, and he considered that Russia had a good chance of development toward socialism without passing through capitalism. We are driven to conclude that Marx regarded his theory of stages merely as a convenient statement of the normal sequence of societies in Western areas; certainly we must regard it in that light . . . . Indeed, Marx in several drafts of a letter, which was never actually sent, to Russian followers, insisted that capitalism had arrived in Western Europe not with the necessity of a law but catastrophically and drew the correct inference that no rules could be laid down for its arrival (he did not mention its departure) there or anywhere else." (Solomon F. Bloom, " Man of His Century: A Reconsideration of the Historical Significance of Karl Marx," *Journal of Political Economy*, December, 1943, p. 496). Of course, Marx and Engels, in the preface to the Russian translation of the *Communist Manifesto* which appeared in 1882, made the following statement: " The purpose of the Communist Manifesto was to proclaim the inescapable and approaching disappearance of the present system of middle-class ownership. In Russia, however, in addition to a feverish development of capitalism and the beginnings of middle-class property ownership, the greater part of the land is to be found in the communal possession of the peasants. The problem is: Can the Russian village community—an already much dilapidated relic of the primitive communal ownership of land—develop directly into a higher Communist type of land ownership, or must it undergo the same dissolution that took place in the historical evolution of the West? The only possible answer today to this question is: If the Russian Revolution is the signal for a workers' revolution in the West, and if these complement one another, then the present-day system of communal ownership in Russia can serve as the starting-point for a Communist development."

But the Russian intelligentsia never saw the *Zukunftsstaat* in the West. It was Peter the Great who predicted that in the long run Russia will have 'to turn its back to Europe'. Stalinism rationalized the ancient belief in peculiar ways of Russian history, and in this new rational cloth adopted this belief as a guiding element in practical politics.

Russia has always been and is in close contact with Asia. While for Western Europe, Russia is Orient, for Asia it is the West. Accused of applying 'Scythian tactics', of being Oriental in Europe, Russia introduced Western methods and ideas in its relations with Asia. Even Bismarck, who always desired to turn Russia eastward in order to get her out of the way of German ambitions in the West, had to admit, 'There in Asia she is a civilizing force'. Pre-revolutionary Russia was civilized overmuch in comparison with Asia and insufficiently in comparison with Europe. From the Bolshevik standpoint Asia, like all colonial and under-developed countries, is, at the present level of technological achievements, more or less in a position to escape the capitalist stage. The Bolsheviks quote Engels' statement that the centre of revolutionary movement is moving to the Orient.

Russia is a world by herself; she is neither Europe nor Asia, but, in a way, belongs to both. Russia always felt and understood Asia better than Europe. The early mercantilist Slavophile Krizânic, who looked for markets for Russia in China, India, Persia, Bukhara; the Smithianist Count Mordinov, who called attention toward India and Persia ('Europe is antiquated; Asia young and uneducated, can tie up closer with Russia'—1816); Pushkin who was not always sure that Russia belonged to Europe, and sometimes considered it a 'mistake of the geographers';[139] the Slavophiles, Pan-Slavists; the later teachings by Danilevski, Leontyev, and the Eurasians—all concur in one way or another with Vladimir Solovyov's Asiatic visions.

In some periods of her history Russia hesitated between the West and the East; but after the revolution of 1917, 'ostracized by Europe—excepting Germany—and America, the Soviet Union naturally looked to Asia to redress the balance: to Asia, where she saw, in the dependent relation of the peoples to the Great Powers, a reflection of her own relations to the class dispossessed by the Revolution. A Congress of Peoples of the East had been organized at Baku in September, 1920, for a holy war against British Imperialism. The Asiatic States were assured of the abandonment by Russia of all unequal privileges secured against them by the

[139] See his letter to Prince Vyazemski of March or April, 1824.

105

Government of the Tsars. Some of them seemed naturally linked to the Soviet Union by a common impulse of social revolution. She seemed at once to be a fellow-sufferer and a champion.'[140]

Again in the tradition of Russian history, the Soviet state developed in its early period a special gravitation toward Asia. It endeavoured to become a magnet, a centre of gravity for the entire world but especially for Asia. 'Borodin's name is Lafayette', said Dr. Sun-Yat-sen, describing the Soviet emissary to the Canton government. This Soviet policy in Asia was in the tradition, for instance, of the old Russian ideas (not the tsarist practice) of 'liberation, not conquest' of India.

The primacy of social over political and economic interests has always been a feature of the Russian people. It has been well understood by German scholars. 'Emphasis on the social is decidedly Russian', says one of the recent investigators; 'to an average Russian, economic problems are identical with social-political problems'.[141] Russian Marxists concentrated on the problem of a just social distribution more than their Western colleagues. The entire history of the Russian intelligentsia is a continuous search for a better *social* order. Political reforms and revolution have been regarded as ways and means to the final goal. It is true that the political side often became an aim in itself, but most of the Decembrists, Slavophiles, Herzen, Bakunin, Lavrov emphasized the primacy of the social element and strove mainly toward a social and not a political revolution. Many were willing to preserve autocracy in case their social aims were achieved. This search for social justice expressed itself in the typically Russian phenomenon of the 'contrite noble', of the rich merchants who would try to pray their sins away, dream of a pilgrimage or of going into a monastery or donating generously toward a socialist revolution. There was no real bourgeois human material in Russia prior to revolution.

This feature of primacy of the social element resulted in two phenomena traditional in Russian history and inherited by the Soviet Union: lack of interest in individual political liberties and absence of individual economic freedom.

The liberal individualism with its political form of parliamentarism never obtained the economic foundation of a developed capitalism in Russia. While no European country grew so visibly in mental stature between 1800 and 1900 as Russia, 'in Russia there are in reality no free people excepting beggars and philoso-

---

[140] Maynard, *The Russian Peasant*, p. 211.
[141] Hans-Jürgen Seraphim, *op. cit.*, pp. 139, 185.

phers', said M. M. Speranski, Herzen stressed that Russia is 'the land of outward slavery and inward freedom'.

Thus the short episode of Russian constitutionalism and of the Duma's functioning had no economic roots in Russian soil. The liberal current, so typical of and dominant in Western Europe of the 19th century, was a Utopia in Russia. And it remained a Utopia after the revolution made possible an escape from capitalism.

In comparing Russia with Western Europe we have to keep in mind that Russia escaped the individualist aspects of the Reformation, of the Renaissance, and of the French Revolution, of parliamentary liberalism.

'In Soviet Communist Russia, on the other hand, there was real freedom because any day might change the life of Russia, and indeed the life of the whole world; it might re-make everything. One day was not just like another. Every young man felt himself a world-builder; the world had become plastic and out of it new forms might be modelled. It was this more than anything which acted on him like a charm. Everyone feels himself a partner in the common business, which has a world-wide significance. Life is absorbed not in the struggle for one's own personal existence but in the reconstruction of the world. So freedom is understood not as liberty of choice, not as liberty to turn to the right nor to the left, but as the active changing of the world, as an act accomplished not by the individual but by the social man, after the choice has been made.'[142]

This idea of a social, collective character of work for the creation of a new world explains the absence of individual economic freedom in Russia in the Western sense. All non-Western societies resent the purely individualist form of economy as contrary to their history and traditions. While in the capitalist form the individual has been the basic unit of economy and the totalitarian regimes present the state as the only base, Russia's vision (as with most Oriental societies) is the 'individual in the collective'.[143]

The infatuation of the Slavophiles and Narodniki with the institutions of mir and artel belong to this conception. That is the idea of *sobornost*, the feeling of the littleness of the individual itself and of strength of the collective, unjustly monopolized by the

---

142 Berdyaev, *op. cit.*, p. 183.

143 See Chapter IV in my *Asia Between Two World Wars*, New York, 1944. Sir John Maynard expressed the same thought in his statement that "Islam, like Eastern Orthodox Christianity, is a social or collectivist religion, in which truth is conceived as residing in the congregation: and 'ijma'a, the consensus of the faithful, takes a place similar to that of *sobornost* in Orthodoxy." *The Russian Peasant*, p. 364.

church, as it presents a feature of general development of Russia, and at the same time a feature common to most non-Western societies. One of the reasons why Marxism conquered Russia was the fact that for Karl Marx the social collective, and not the individual was the centre of his teachings. As we have seen, there was no sympathy for the English classical school in Russia. Typically, Dostoyevski wrote in his testimony to the commission investigating the Petrashevski affair. 'Socialism is the same political economy but just in a different form'. Even Russian Westernism was mostly of the Oriental type: acceptance of technological advances but not of the social forms.

Belinski's emphasis on 'sociality' as his slogan is typical of the Russian climate. In the Soviet Union the atmosphere is full of the feeling of *sobornost,* and, speaking with Sir John Maynard, even 'the *Mir* dipped under the surface, and again reappeared in the form of a Collective Farm Committee'. The development of the Russian theatre (witness the theories and practice of the Moscow Art Theatre) is a typical manifestation of the Russian trend of coercion of the individual into teamwork.

The centre of Russian early socialism was the peasant; of orthodox Marxism, the factory worker. But in Russia most of the factory workers were, prior to the revolution, still tied up with the village. Russian Marxism encountered opposition on the part of strong Populist agrarian socialist currents. For Russian socialists the peasant was what the proletariat was in the West. A Frenchman of the end of the 18th century stated, speaking of Russia: 'The third estate does not exist, neither the bourgeois nor the merchant, properly speaking; with the exception of the clergy, the nobility, and the military class, everybody is *mushick, i.e.* a serf.'[144] This Rousseauism remained for a long time true to the history of Russia. Hence the 'going into the People' movements, hence the idealization of the peasant by revolutionary groups in Russia. Marxism broke up the idea of Russia as a peasant kingdom. Lenin's genius, of course, took into consideration the role of the peasant ('Land and Peace' was his first battle cry). But the Soviet Union gave up the idealization and idolization of the factory worker as well as of the peasant, putting both of them through the mill of intensive industrialization. And inasmuch as the numerically small nobility and bourgeoisie no longer existed, the Soviet Union united the nation, identifying it with the all-embracing working class.

[144] Jean Benoit Sherer. *Histoire raisonnée du commerce de la Russie,* Paris, 1788, Vol. I, pp. 104f.

Hatred of the bourgeoisie was not a Bolshevik invention either. 'An anti-capitalist, anti-bourgeois attitude developed very early in Russia, and not only among the radicals'.[145] Russian intelligentsia and revolutionary youth for one hundred years could not find a more despised expression than 'petty bourgeoisie' *(meshshanstvo).* We recollect from previous chapters that Botkin's prayer 'Lord, give us a bourgeoisie' was a unique exception which found later allies only in Russian revisionists. Herzen was one of the most violent and eloquent haters of the bourgeoisie; Chernyshevski joined him; the nihilists added fire to the old hatred.

The revolution of 1917 was accused of a violence of destruction. Whoever witnessed and remembers the period of military dictatorship of the proletariat and the period of civil war, when Bolshevism challenged state, religion, patriotism, private property, family, is certainly ready to emphasize the violence of the revolution. It was truly a picture reminiscent of the 'huge, mischievous, hundred mouthed monster'. But was this greatness and violence of destruction an invention of the revolution?

The physiocrat Mercier de la Rivière foresaw it when he wrote on October 19, 1767, from St. Petersburg to his friend Abbé Raynal in Paris, that in Russia *'tout est à defaire et à refaire'.* Pushkin's fear of a 'Russian rebellion, insane and ruthless' is still fresh in our memories. The Russian Fourierists preached the necessity to 'destroy capitals, cities, and apply all their materials for other purposes' (I quote from speeches at the celebration of Fourier's birthday by the Petrashevski circle). We remember the Russian nihilists of whom Nietzsche said once: 'I observe more inclination toward greatness in the feelings of the Russian nihilists than in those of the English utilitarians'. The young Bakunin formulated this tradition in his famous statement: *Die Lust der Zerstörung ist zugleich eine schaffende Lust.*[146] Professor V. Pecherin, later converted to Catholicism, expressed the same thought even more drastically:

> How sweet it is to hate one's native land
> Eagerly awaiting its destruction,
> And in the destruction of the fatherland
> To see the dawn of world awakening.

The grand style of destruction was constantly accompanied by

145 Frederick Charles Barghoorn, " The Russian Radicals of the 1860's and the Problem of the Industrial Proletariat " in *Slavonic and East European Review,* March, 1943, p. 57.

146 In the article *"Die Reaktion in Deutschland, Ein Fragment von Einem Franzosen,"* signed Jules Elysard and introduced by Ruge, *Deutsche Jahrbücher für Wissenschaft und Kunst,* October 17-21, 1842.

a grand style of creation, by grandiose plans of reconstruction, especially in the economic field. The great Russian historian S. M. Solovyov emphasized how old Russia 'had first of all to get out of economic bankruptcy, to enrich and strengthen itself' in the same way as the Bolsheviks preached that it was imperative to 'catch and overtake' Western industrialism. The just-quoted speeches at the celebration of Fourier's birthday contained a constructive programme 'to cover the entire poor earth with palaces, fruit, and flowers. We here in our country will start the reconstruction, and the entire world will finish it.' It seems that Heinrich Heine overheard these speeches:

> Wir wollen hier auf Erden schon
> Das Himmelreich errichten.

Russian schemes of creation have always been full of a *furor technicus*. Enemies of the revolution liked to cite that in the first years after 1917 one could see a sign on the door of the Commission of Electrification: 'Please knock. The bell doesn't work'; they considered it typical and symbolic of the Soviet Union as well as of old Russia. Actually, ideas of technological innovations and advancement as associated with social progress are an old tradition of the Russian intelligentsia. The 'thinking realist' Pisarev stressed it. The Utopias by Prince V. F. Odoyevski, the published one [147] as well as the numerous fragments of the third part of his unfinished *Russian Nights*, are typical of this socio-technological trend. Exceeding Jules Verne in imagination, but lacking any conciseness of plot, full of a combination of technological revolution and social progress, this Utopia crowns the main idea of Odoyevski's trilogy picturing the coming complete conquest of the forces of nature by mankind. It emphasizes that this process started in Russia with the reforms of Peter the Great, and that human progress is inseparable from progress of science. Remarkable pages are dedicated to the description (by Chartin, 'Historian ordinarius at the office of the First Poet of the Army') of the future scientific organization in Russia which combines and interrelates disciplines usually artificially separated and isolated. It sounds today almost like a prediction of the present role of science in the Soviet Union.[148]

---

[147] V. F. Odoyevski, "Two Days in the Life of the Earth" (signed "Kallidor") in the *Moscow Messenger*, 1828; also "The Year 4338, Letters from St. Petersburg from Ippolit Zungiev, Student of the Main School at Peking to Lingin, Student of the Same School," in the almanac *Dawn* for 1840. The last was a fragment from his trilogy.

[148] See "The Soviet Way; Integrated Research is Made to Serve a State at War," *New York Times*, November 7, 1943. It shows "how every

The conviction of man's ability to make history, to be subject and not object of development, and the belief in daring experimentation are closely interwoven with the traditional Russian striving toward technological innovations. Peter the Great was the author of the first Five Year Plan. Belinski used to state that often in Russia things can be done in five years which in the West would require fifty years. Herzen concurred in this opinion. Russian radical youth of the beginning of the 20th century was brought up on Bogdanov's *Red Star*, and youngsters and oldsters in the Soviet Union still enjoy the delightful *Aelita* by Alexey Tolstoy. Even the poetical Utopias by the poet of the revolution, Mayakovski, are full of the *furor technicus.*

N. K. Mikhailovski called attention to the unusual advantages of the lag in Russia's civilization which should enable the country to use the lessons of other peoples' history and their technological knowledge for deliberately directing its own course of development. The Bolsheviks adopted the same view and proved the thesis that at present Utopias are much more capable of being carried out than has so far been believed; that adoption and development of technology makes it possible to plot the curve of history ahead; that 'Fate was no longer Fate' (Maynard).

The development of the Soviet Union is a successful illustration of the theory of 'jumps', or short cuts. The ideal of slow, gradual progress did not seem to succeed in Russia. The Russians always preferred to work by fits and starts and not by steady, sustained pull. This working in spurts was systematized and utilized by the Soviet system. The famous *Stakhanovshchina* is nothing else than an able utilization of it. The same type of work is being applied to the development of the country as a whole. 'Jumps' are considered an essential of evolution: slow changes prepare the ground for the jumps; jumps open the road for further slow changes.

The internal organization and climate of the ruling Communist party are also along the traditional lines of Russian history. We became acquainted in previous pages with Russian circles, conspiracies, secret societies, and revolutionary groups. We became acquainted with the type of an almost professional revolutionary, Bakunin. The revolution of 1917 opened a field of constructive work to the destroyers of bourgeois society, and they successfully

---

scientific institution, from the Academy of Science at the top to the lowliest factory laboratory, is meshed into a single colossal system. . . . Theory and practice are now so interwoven that separation is scarcely possible. . . . The reason for the remarkable showing is that Soviet Russia is the only nation in the world which has a plan for the integration and systematic exploitation of all sciences."

replaced after years of trials and errors—the pre-revolutionary centralized bureaucracy. They became the 'serving people' (*slushiliye lyudi*) who served at the court of old Russia, in the army, in the administrative offices.

In this new type of activity the former revolutionaries, now the rulers, preserved the old, almost religious fervour and faith of a sect,[149] applying it to electrification of the country, to building industrial plants, to introduction of agricultural machinery, organization of statistics and accounting, and so on. How different were the Russian Bolsheviks from the orthodox German socialists with their dull life and passionless orderly organization!

The system of government by coercion is certainly traditional in Russian history. The Russian intelligentsia realized it and, as we have seen in previous chapters, hoped for 'reforms from above'. In order to realize his reform plans, Krizânic hoped to be appointed court librarian and adviser to Tsar Alexy.[150] Kotoshikhin claimed that the Tsar holds Moses' rod. Collaborators of Peter the Great emphasized that Russians have to be coerced to actions necessary for their own welfare. Chaadayev desired to become adviser and philosopher to the state; Pushkin wanted to see reforms 'at a wave of the Tsar's hand' and speaking of Peter the Great in the famous Stanzas, praised his courageous introduction of education by autocratic methods. Admiration for Peter the Great (Belinski, Chernyshevski) influenced the spread of the opinion among the Westerners that great reforms could be initiated in Russia only from above. Herzen [151] and Mikhailovski sometimes, and the

---

[149] It is rather interesting that many of the forefathers of the Russian revolution, like Dobrolyubov, Chernyshevski, and others, were sons of priests. Stalin, too, was educated in a theological seminary. Sir John Maynard carries the parallel too far in comparing the organization of the party with the Orthodox Church. "Even the Party—that unique misnomer of the vocation of leadership—is not really new: but rather a new application of an ancient institution—the priesthood. Think of it as a lay Church: beside which all rivals are but heretics: having a monopoly of teaching, supplying the personnel of many offices of State, as the Mediaeval Church did: bound to certain abstentions, as were the mediaeval Churchmen: accessible to ability from all social strata, as was the Church: marked off from the rest by the dedication to particular tasks, as were the priests: liable to be unfrocked, as perhaps the Churchmen were not. The parallel extends even to significant details such as the markings of the head and by the shaving of a portion of it. The Communist shaves the face as the priest shaved the crown." (*The Russian Peasant*, pp. 20-21.) Peter the Great mocked the church, but there was religious fervour in his work.

[150] Adam Olearius who visited Moscow at that time called it *Monarchia dominica et despotica*.

[151] Herzen characterized Peter the Great as a "revolutionary terrorist". Klyuchevski seconded him, stating that Peter I's "beneficent actions were accomplished with repelling violence".

Slavophiles usually, shared this opinion. The idea of omnipotence of the state is reflected in Saltykov-Shchedrin's *A Complicated Affair* when socialist tendencies are expressed in the form of a poor functionary's dream.

The Bolsheviks remained faithful to this tradition. They seemed to have excellent knowledge of the nature and psychology of the Russians. An erudite agronomist, secretary of the Imperial Moscow Agricultural Society, said once, speaking of public works in Russia: 'If ordered—nothing is impossible for a Russian'.[152] The foundation of St. Petersburg on marshes, in complete isolation from the country, on the frontier, with no food supply near, is typical of the hurricane changes by order.

The transfer of the capital after the revolution of 1917 from St. Petersburg to Moscow was not a Bolshevik invention; some of the Decembrists considered the transfer to Moscow or Nizhni Novgorod; the Slavophiles dreamed of it; Herzen predicted it in 1853.

I could continue this list of parallels, with features like dogmatism and intolerance, the tendency toward isolation,[153] absence of pedantism, and the breaking of rules in adjusting to changed situations, which all present fruitful illustrations of the suggested thesis. But it seems to me that the case does not require additional quantitative strengthening.

Novelties may tickle the conscious curiosity; but the deeper levels are stirred by older impulses, whose echoes go back to the childhood of the individual and the nation.

A strong feeling of history unites the Soviet Union with pre-revolutionary Russia; and again I agree with Sir John Maynard when he says of Bolsheviks that 'these revolutionaries have a sense of continuity of history and of their inheritance from the past'.

The Bolsheviks have ceased to believe that history began on October 25, 1917.[154] They not only returned to the Germans and to the entire world the advice given in 1918 by the German publicist Maximilian Harden ('Read Russian history. It is a highly useful occupation') but they themselves followed this advice. They are eagerly rediscovering their past; and again this metamorphosis follows the tradition of the Russian intelligentsia. What the Bol-

---

[152] Maslov in *Agricultural Journal*, 1836, p. 146, quoted by Peter Struve, in *Serf Economy*, St. Petersburg, 1913, p. 209.

[153] It was Križanic who said: "Closing of the frontiers represents the heart and soul of the Russian state". A besieged city or a besieged island is, for the time being, always communist. Was not the early Soviet state under blockade by former Russian allies?

[154] Comte de Ségur stated in 1789: "This is the year one in history."

sheviks rediscovered is not the conservative reactionary historism formulated by the boyar Bersen Beklemishev; it is not the sentimental evocation of the Russian past occasionally expressed by the Decembrists and the Westerners. The present historism is distinct from the longing for the *kvas* and *poddyovka* (national costume— a kind of sleeveless overcoat) of the Slavophiles. I think the historism of the Bolsheviks is in line with the formula suggested by the Decembrist Mikhail S. Lunin, who wrote from his prison in Siberia: 'History is necessary not only for curiosity and speculations but to guide us in the high domain of politics.' When Pushkin, the *frondeur,* the poet of liberty, the author of inspiring revolutionary poetry, began the study of archive materials for his *History of the Pugachev Revolt,* for his *Boris Godunov,* and in the preparation for the intended history of Peter the Great, he changed into a defender of Russian nationalism. His prophetic *To the Slanderers of Russia* sounds contemporary today.[155] Soviet critics stress Pushkin's historism as an adaptation of a peculiarly Russian strain.[156]

The new fashionable Russian historism is not an artificial attempt to harness old horses to the Soviet machine. Lenin himself always insisted on preservation of the past, preaching that even 'bricks of capitalism' should be saved for the foundation of the new structure. The return to historism in the Soviet Union did not occur overnight: it happened after a bitter fight against Pokrovski's historical school and against extremes of Marxian formalism in economics. It received its final baptism in Stalin's emphasis that Soviet literature and life must be 'proletarian in content and national in form', in the revision of history textbooks and historical methods,[157] in the reform of economic teaching.[158] Thus the Soviet

[155] One can find an interesting statement on Russian nationalism in the forgotten *Thoughts on Russia* by A. Krayevski: "We are not Europeans, but not Asiatics either. . . . We are Russians, inhabitants of the one-sixth of the earth called Russia." Literary Supplement to the *Russian Invalid,* 1837, No. 2, p. 9.

[156] See especially I. Vinogradov, "Pushkin's Road to Realism" in *Pushkin, Homage by Marxian Critics* (English translation), New York, 1937.

[157] See *Against Pokrovski's Historical Conception;* Collection of Essays edited by the Institute of History of the Academy of Science, 2 volumes, Leningrad, 1939.

[158] The intensive discussion in the United States press of the alleged Soviet abandonment of Marxian economics based on an article by L. A. Leontyev in "Under the Banner of Marxism" (1943) is just a product of wishful thinking. The article represents a new emphasis on the historical elements of economic development. One can find similar criticism of teaching of economics in the Soviet Union in articles by A. I. Stetski, "On Institutes of Red Professors," *Bolshevik,* December, 1935, and A. Pashkov, "Political Economy in the Broad Meaning of the Word," *Under the Banner of Marxism,* January, 1936.

Union in the traditional Russian way turned its face toward national history.

World War II accelerated and strengthened the metamorphosis in the same way as the result of World War I tended to de-historize and de-nationalize the Russian mind. The magnetic inspiration of its own history, of generations of ancestors, began to work its spell on the Soviet people.

Alexey Tolstoy's explanation of the newly developed historism in the literature of the lands of the Soviets can be fully applied to the 'new-old' trends in social and economic thought. 'It is no accident that in Soviet literature there has been such a wide development of the historical novel. . . .And for the first time, like the voice of the bell of the city of Kitezh, there has sounded in Soviet literature the words: sacred motherland.'[159]

The Soviet peoples recalled and became inspired by the events of 1812 not less than by Peter the Great's fight against Sweden when this country, then the strongest power of Europe, was defeated thanks to accelerated industrialization, which, as at present, was concentrated in the Urals. They recall Pushkin's statement made some one hundred and twenty years ago: 'Russia entered Europe like a newly launched ship, to the noise of a hammer and the thunder of guns'.

The events of World War II testified that there are not Old and New Russia: it is always Russia.

---

[159] Alexey Tolstoy, *op. cit.*

H

# VII. Conclusions

THE musical fugue of the development of Russian economic thought has come to a close. All the voices which entered the field followed one another, co-existed, interrelated, contributed to the general construction of the fugue even through their fights for dominance, and led to the last chord, whose harmony crowns the musical fugue. This last chord was Bolshevism, which became the expression of Russian socialism.

Our rapid turning through the score of Russian history was intended to give us a sense of thematic structure, and to bring some small degree of order into our understanding of the so-called chaos of Russian economics.

In 1917 a section of Russian history ended; and while some were eager to turn the page, others would gladly have delayed its turning.

Like every new economic form, Bolshevism, at its coming, seemed a monster, to whom people turned their eyes in hatred or bewilderment. Cassandras and Jeremiahs spoke of it as Othello does to Desdemona:

> . . . of the Cannibals that each other eat,
> The Anthropofagi and men whose heads
> Do grow beneath their shoulders.

To some, on the other side of the fence, the coming of Bolshevism was equivalent to the advent of the messiah, to the beginning of paradise on earth. They greeted the fulfillment of their Utopia. In this connection we may well recall Aristotle's illustration: that from the same letters of the alphabet either a comedy or a tragedy might emerge.

When an earthquake occurs, its waves start far below the ground and travel in all directions. When they finally emerge at the surface, changes become visible. From the standpoint of Russian history, Bolshevism should be viewed as a legitimate successor rather than a successful rebel. Its dramatic suddenness struck only contemporaries. It is true that the world prior to 1917 is gone forever, as the world of 1789 vanished after the French Revolution. Taken singly, the events of 1917 have appeared sometimes irrational and often causeless. Viewed in a historical succession, they are seen to have been governed by logic and consistency; they present a cumulative effect of developments scarcely noticed at an earlier time. History of economic ideas is not a chain of separate links but an unceasing stream. This stream absorbed foreign influences as well as native currents; conservative and revolutionary ideas. All of them went into the channel of continuous Russian history, whose waters have shaped and filled the Soviet construction of that Marxian theoretical canal system which for decades fescinated the Russian intelligentsia.

The Bolshevism of 1917, with its strong Marxian basis, compounded in the chemical retorts of Russian history, processed in the horrors of the civil war and World War II, appears today as the Russian socialism. Just as capitalism is not uniform throughout Western civilization, but has its local, national, and historical colourings, so it is with socialism. Russian socialism, in its early epic forms of social titanism or in its present forms of sober working bureaucracy, differs from defunct German Social Democracy as well as from elemental French syndicalism or from conventional English labour thought.

It was not the Communist party, not the Politbureau, not Stalin who performed the joining of Marxian theory with the needs and traditions of Russia. The ship of state returns to its historical channel sometimes without a skipper, sometimes against the skipper's wish. To Stalin's credit, he did not try to stop the process. It is a manifestation of the statement that dialectical materialism is false to its own nature when it becomes dogmatic.

Russian socialism became a mass phenomenon, a national phenomenon. This fact is more important than an eventual reconciliation and patching-up of factional schisms. Pushkin's tragedy *Boris Godunov*, a picture of disputed successions, ends laconically with a stage direction: 'The people is silent'. People in history, like the chorus in a Greek tragedy, have the first word and the last one. The Russian people has not remained silent this time. The defence of Stalingrad was its answer.

One has to admit that the new social order in the Soviet Union, highly collectivized, is admirably suited to war requirements. It is full of readiness to experiment and full of revolutionary toughness. The Soviet system with its discipline, common effort, permanent public service, and constant deprivations was certainly a good school for war preparation. No wonder the Soviet civilization appeared robust and vigorous when put to test in the last world war.

117

The spirit of Russian economics was for one hundred years one of quest for transformation. It has changed: conservation is its prime goal at present, conservation of the conquests of the revolution, conservation of its creative work, conservation of its industrialized and to-be-industrialized territories. The Soviet Union is sacrificing human lives and accumulated assets to conserve its *status quo* and its work of reconstruction. The Soviet conception is that the U.S.S.R. has solved the problem of social organization, that she has solved the problems of relations between men in the economic process, that her citizens have to work only on the conquest of nature. The constant lag in Russian history between economic development and social structure, between industrial and military power, disappeared.

A Dutch proverb says: To make a man conservative, give him something to conserve. The people of the Soviet Union still have the dynamic impulse of a successful revolution, but their economic spirit is obviously one of conservation. It is the conservative spirit of *beati possidentes* contrasting with quest for transformation by the discontented in 1917.[160]

Herein lies the present distinction between Western civilization and the Soviet Union. For the sake of national interests and those of mankind, for the sake of unhindered development of her natural resources and productive forces, for the sake of fulfillment of her 'historical mission' on the earth, the Soviet Union had to adopt the principle of conservation. The optimism of the Russian present quest for conservation contrasts with the pessimism of the Western attempts at conservation of the *status quo*. The 20th century is at the same time a solving and a dissolving epoch. The Russians are certain they have reached the solving stage: hence their feverish conservation trend. For the Russians it is at present a battle for the *conservation of the transformation which already has been carried through in their country*.

And the prognosis?

Beginning and end are always a mystery. We cannot spy out the land of the future; its boundaries are unknown. We cannot give a name to an unknown era and to a realm yet unlived. New principles and concepts are taking shape under our very eyes, even though tumultuously; and here and there are thrown the shadows of what may come. We look wonderingly and fearfully into the future, and the road is icy and treacherous.

Each revolution is a judgment within history. The judgment of history approved of the October Revolution. Nevertheless, for a

[160] *Spirit of American Economics*, pp. 31f.

long time the Russians will still have to live in the troposphere enwrapping the earth, in the sphere of change, winds, and storms, dreaming of the perfect calmness of the stratosphere where storms cannot penetrate. The world is still between the two epochs. But the Russians will preserve their pathos of creation and their romanticism of realism, romanticism of a system which in Lenin's definition consists of 'Soviets, electricity, and accounting'.[161]

I am not sure that near history will allow the Russians to say, in the beautiful cadence of Shakespeare's sonnet, 'all losses are restored and sorrows end' (they were warned years ago against 'giddiness from success'); but many would wish to have been born late enough to enjoy the experience of future generations in the Soviet Union.

[161] Cf. R. J. Kerner, *The Russian Adventure*, University of California Press, 1943.

# Bibliographical Note

No scholarly attempt has yet been made to study the development of Russian economic thought as a whole.

Typically for economically later developed countries we find in Russia—as in the case of the United States—a denial by academic economists of the very existence of native economic thought. V. P. Bezobrazov went so far in this denial as to declare that all economic theories originating on Russian soil *'n'offrent toutefois aucune importance dans le progrès général de la science'*.[162] N. Ch. Bunge, one of the most erudite and truly academic Russian economists, who was curious enough to study the American dissenters Henry Carey and Henry George, and possessed an unusual knowledge of world economic literature in regard to Russia, remarked: *'Notre littérature n'à pas donné naissance à des doctrines économiques nouvelles'*.[163]

The conception was generally accepted in Russia that political conditions prevented a free development of economic and social thought in the country. Bezobrazov, one of the most active and industrious among the neglected Russian economists, suggested this explanation in his report to the Academy of Sciences. Describing the progress of the discipline in the West he observed: *'Chez nous, rien de pareil s'est produit'*. He was indignant that the most remarkable economic studies on Russia were published by foreigners, and regarded the work of Storch, his predecessor at the academy, as belonging more to the West than to Russia, emphasizing that Storch's course could not even be published in Russian on account of the censorship.[164] And exactly fifty years later another member of the Academy of Sciences, A. S. Lappo-

---

[162] *De l'influence de la science économique sur la vie de l'Europe moderne"* in *Memoires de l'Academie Impériale des Sciences de Saint-Petersbourg.* Serie VII. Vol. XI, St. Petersburg, 1867, p. 77. Bezobrazov extends this judgment by way of illustration to writers like Pososhkov, Krankrin, and especially Nicolas Turgeney.

[163] *Esquisses de littérature politico-économique.* French translation, Genève, 1897, p. 191. The original Russian edition of 1895 was not available at the time of writing. Bunge admits only the importance of some historico-statistical material collected in Russia especially by the *zemstvos.* Unfortunately Bunge did not fulfil his promise to prepare a chapter on Russian economics for the intended second volume of his *Esquisses.*

[164] *Op. cit.,* p. 77.

Danilevski, in an English study repeated the same explanation: 'Political circumstances were not favourable'.[165] And even after the revolution of 1917 N. D. Kondratyev stressed that 'in the field of economics Russia is just entering upon the world stage'[166]

On the other hand, deeply involved in their eternal discussions of the fate of capitalism, of the future of the economic structure, of the coming social revolution, Russian economists obviously developed a lack of interest in *Dogmengeschichte*. Similarly in the United States it was fashionable to refer to the difficulty of writing history 'on the march'.

The few Russian attempts to sketch the evolution of Russian economic thought are limited to a speech by V. N. Leshkov,[167] fragmentary essays by V. V. Svyatlovski,[168] and a superficial study on development of socialist ideas in Russia by M. A. Pashitnov.[169]

No Russian encyclopedia (the popular Brockhaus-Efron and the Great Soviet Encyclopedia included) ever tried to survey the field of Russian economics.

No more successful was the discussion of Russian economics in foreign languages, with the exception of German. The attempts in English are restricted to the above mentioned formal brief report for non-Russians by a non-economist, A. S. Lappo-Danilevski, in his English discussion *Science and Learning in Russia,* to a superficial article by A. N. Miklashevski in *Palgrave's Dictionary,* and a surprisingly unsatisfactory sketch by P. B. Struve in the *Encyclopedia of the Social Sciences.* The industrious Luigi Cossa included few pages on Russian economics between sketches on Finland and Hungary in his *History of Economic Doctrines.*[170] But it is just an incidental enumeration of wrongly spelled names.

The Germans diligently tried to trace and follow up the development of economic thought in Russia. The case is even more extreme than that of German interest in American economics. While a systematic, exhaustive study is missing even in German literature, continuous and persistent attempts have been undertaken to investigate the trends of Russian thought, to penetrate the Russian mind. Wilhelm Roscher's report on his discovery of a

165 " Science and Learning in Russia " in *Russian Realities and Problems* edited by J. D. Duff, Cambridge. England, 1917, p. 172.

166 *Mikhail Ivanovitch Tugan-Baranovski,* Petrograd, 1923, p. 113.

167 "The Ancient Russian Science of National Wealth and Welfare" in *Memoir of January 12, 1855* (Centenary of the University of Moscow), Moscow, 1855.

168 *Contributions to the History of Political Economy and Statistics in Russia.* St. Petersburg, 1906.

169 *Evolution of Socialist Ideas in Russia,* Vol. I, Kharkov, 1913.

170 French translation, Paris, 1899. 453-459.

German-Russian school of economics was published in 1870,[171] but the contemporary German economist Hans-Jürgen Seraphim in a monograph published in 1925 is still setting forth an argument against Roscher's theory.[172] As in the American case, Russian economists themselves undertook an inventory of their discipline only upon German initiative and request. Thus we encounter in the known collection *Die Wirtschaftstheorie der Gegenwart* uneven and unbalanced surveys by Vladimir Y. Zheleznov[173] and Dimitri N. Ivantsov.[174]

The German literature presents a mass of monographs and dissertations on Russian economists and statesmen and their theories. There are not many Russian theorists of importance left whose *volkswirtschaftliche Anschauungen* have not served as a topic for a Ph.D. thesis in a German university.

The Germans undertook a systematic study of the special domain of Russian economics in which the Russians were successful and influential on a world scale—the investigation of business cycles.[175] Russian mercantilism, Russian Populism, Russian anarchism also found diligent attention in German literature. Hans-Jürgen Seraphim is correct in emphasizing the fragmentary character of all these undertakings, but he is certainly wrong in deploring the lack of information in Germany concerning the 'independent Russian *Sozialökonomie* since the middle of the 19th century':[176] after that time the German influence was growing, and practically no independent Russian economic thought existed.

The motives for German interest are clear: in addition to the generally prevailing historical character of German economics there were important factors of geographical proximity, historical and social intercourse of a constant elbow-rubbing with the Germans, as well as the fact of predominance for a long time of German economic ideas and economic influence. German universities trained Russian economists; German periodicals opened their pages to the products of their pens; many of the violent Russian polemics were published in German academic and socialist periodicals.

The U.S.S.R. for a long time discarded pre-Soviet economics. But slowly the new 'historism' changed the situation. The intensive

---

[171] *" Die Deutsch-Russische Schule "* in *Berichte der Königlich Sächsischen Gesellschaft der Wissenschaften zu Leipzig*, 1870, Vol. 2.

[172] *Neuere Russische Wert- und Kapitalzinstheorien*, Berlin u. Leipzig, 1925 (*Sozialwissenschaftliche Forschungen, Abt. I, Heft 4*).

[173] Vol. I. Wien, 1927.

[174] Vol. IV. Wien, 1928.

[175] Ralph Wagenführ, *Die Konjunkturtheorie in Russland*, Jena, 1929.

[176] *Op. cit.*, p. 9.

excavation of Russian archives began to bear fruit, and Soviet literature turned its attention to the history of ideas. The publication of *Sketches of Economic Thought in Russia in the First Half of the 19th Century* by I. G. Blyumin[177] is an illustration of this trend. Unfortunately this study, abundant of material, simplifies the evolution, applying orthodox schemes and using conventional jargon.

The literature on socialism and communism is immense, and bibliographies are numerous.

[177] Leningrad, 1940.

# Index